Praise for *Running Uphill*

"Harry Jerome is Canada's Jessie Owens. He faced the same battles in his time as Jessie did. Frankly, Harry Jerome's face should be on a dollar bill. He should be a national hero for what he went through."

—Donovan Bailey, five-time world and Olympic champion

"Having known Fil Fraser from the earliest days of my career, I have always been struck by his humanity, which knew no differences based on race, colour, creed or any other differentiating factor. Having said that, he knows only too well the struggles of many ethnic groups—including his and my own— to find an equal place in the Canadian firmament. Harry Jerome, who was approximately my contemporary, was one of those who got out ahead of the pack and paid a price. What a fitting biographer Fil Fraser is. I applaud his compassion and his art."

—Michael A. Levine, entertainment lawyer, Goodmans LLP

"Harry Jerome was, of course, a great athlete. When I watched Harry run, it seemed as if he was floating. I am extremely happy to see this book published in honour of the fastest man in the world. It was about time."

—John Braithwaite, former city councillor, City of North Vancouver

"My congratulations to Fil Fraser; a book on Harry Jerome is long overdue. Fil Fraser grippingly captures the essence of Harry's character and how his life's experiences factor into the development of his indomitable spirit, athletic achievement and desire to assist Canadian sports and society to be better. An inspiring recounting of a great Canadian's achievements."

–Milton K. Wong, Chair, HSBC Asset
Management Canada

"All of us need to know the stories of our Black ancestors to breathe us across those extremely tough finish lines—or just to help us survive with dignity. Fil Fraser has generously, with clarity, passion and intellectual rigour, given us the story of our stellar and little-known ancestor Harry Jerome. Breathe in Jerome's energy, breathe out defeat."

–Rita Shelton Deverell, CM, EdD,
CanWest Global Fellow (Winter 2007),
University of Western Ontario

"Too often, we neglect to immortalize our eminent heroes. Fil Fraser has done a superb job of capturing the spirit of Harry Jerome, the flavour of the hostile social climate in which he lived and the significance of his triumphs."

–B. Denham Jolly, president & CEO,
Milestone Radio

"Fil Fraser has provided us with a rich account of the too-brief life of Harry Jerome. Every Black person living in Canada owes a debt of gratitude to Fil Fraser for introducing us to Harry Jerome—someone who was not only a great athlete and an unblemished hero, but also a positive role model for many of us who lament the dearth of Black role models in this country. Every young person, regardless of race, should read this book. It will certainly be a real source of inspiration for decades to come."

–Dr. W. Andy Knight, professor,
University of Alberta

"*Running Uphill* showcases Harry Jerome's race upon the treadmill of "race," where progress against racism is glacial, even for an Olympic sprinter. Fil Fraser explains this pernicious irony, this very Canadian paradox, in masterful, beautiful prose. His humour is a razor; his honesty is a guillotine. In Fraser's bio, heroic Jerome looms larger than life—and too fast for anyone to weight him down with labels.

–George Elliott Clarke, Laureate, 2005–08,
Pierre Elliott Trudeau Fellowship Prize

This meticulous study of the brief life and career of Harry Jerome represents an important milestone in Canadian publishing. We are growing up and recognizing that significant numbers of Canadians of non-European descent have been making contributions to this country's greatness for more than a hundred years, and doing so against the odds.

Harry Jerome's life has the earmarks of many powerful stories—he wins our hearts, he breaks our hearts and he dies too soon. If he had lived to complete his journey from vulnerability to confidence, from frailty to strength, he would have seen that he is finally being given his due in a country that is famous for its ambivalence toward its own heroes and successes.

An influential figure in Canadian broadcasting and policymaking, Fil Fraser has brought the complexities of Black Canadian life, and his own life, to the writing of this important book. Without glossing over Jerome's failings and weaknesses, Fraser has told this story with the honesty and tenderness that Harry Jerome deserves.

—Cheryl Foggo, author, filmmaker and historian

RUNNING UPHILL

The Fast, Short Life of
Canadian Champion Harry Jerome

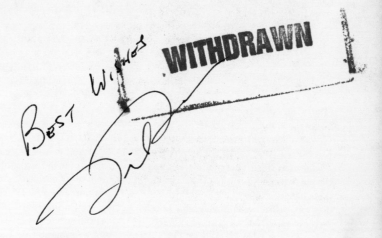

Fil Fraser

DRAGON
HILL

The Publisher: Dragon Hill Publishing Ltd.
www.dragonhillpublishing.com

Library and Archives Canada Cataloguing in Publication

Fraser, Fil, 1932–
  Running uphill : the fast, short life of Canadian champion Harry Jerome / Fil Fraser.

ISBN 13: 978-1-896124-13-1
ISBN 10: 1-896124-13-5

  1. Jerome, Harry, 1940–1982. 2. Runners (Sports)—Canada—Biography.
3. Black Canadians—Biography. I. Title.

GV1061.15.J47F73 2006   796.42092   C2007-901382-1

Project Director: Gary Whyte
Cover photo: Bill Cunningham, *Vancouver Province*
Chapter quotations: from *Dreams from My Father*, by Barack Obama. New York: Three Rivers Press, 1995, 2004. Used with permission.
Photography credits: Every effort has been made to determine the holder of copyright for the photographs in this book. Please inform the publisher of any errors or omissions so that changes can be made in future editions. *Photos courtesy of* AP Wirephoto (p. 133, df60950 Aus); Bata Shoe Museum, Toronto (p. 210); Bill Cunningham, *Vancouver Province* (pp. 59, 77, 83, 96, 173); The Chancellery, Government of Canada (p. 189); Gordon Sedawie, *Vancouver Province* (p. 190); McDonald/CP Wirephoto (p. 84); Metropolitan Photos (p. 69, FM-3-7941); Mike Turk (p. 176, LE3-3107); National Health and Welfare Information Services Canada (p. 109, 70-00106; p. 168, 70-00142; p. 187, 70-00143; p. 193, 70-00138); *Ottawa Citizen* (p. 158); Paul Winn (p. 113); Susan Philips (p. 40, 116); Wendy Jerome (pp. 15, 30, 32, 35, 42, 47, 51, 54, 56, 63, 66, 71, 73, 80, 85, 87, 89, 91, 93, 100, 103, 107, 119, 129, 146, 149, 155, 163, 170, 181, 185, 187, 197, 205, 209, 212, 221).

The author acknowledges the financial support of the Alberta Foundation for the Arts.

PC: P5

Table of Contents

Dedication

This book is dedicated to the memory of my brother, Francis (Frank) Malcolm Blache Fraser (1935–2004), who played professional football in the CFL and who, like Harry Jerome, ran uphill—and succeeded.

Acknowledgements

Writers write alone, but no writer is alone. We are bolstered by the stuff of our lives; the memories from which we mine information and anecdotes, inspiration and insight, and by our real life environments: family, mentors, supporters, editors, publishers and patrons, those individuals and agencies who support the arts.

I want to express my deep thanks to Denham Jolly, who encouraged me to write this book and provided early material support. Paul Winn and Wendy Jerome were my most helpful and cooperative sources of information. Many of Harry Jerome's friends and family were generous in answering questions that sometimes evoked painful memories. Dr. Brian Maraj and Dr. Ruth Morey-Sorrentino provided valuable insights into the challenges faced by elite track athletes.

Thanks to my editor, Nicholle for her careful work, and to Ken, who believed in the book from the very beginning. Thank you, too, to the Alberta Foundation for the Arts, which has, for the second time, supported my book writing adventure.

My wife, Gladys Odegard, continues to surround me with an atmosphere of unqualified support that makes my life a dream.

Foreword by Paul Winn[1]

Running Uphill is the story of the life of my friend Harry Winston Jerome and is long overdue. As I read through it, I couldn't help but think that had he been white, the book would have been written sooner.

Many memories of my friendship with Harry came rushing back, reminding me of the kind of world we lived in as teenagers. The late 1950s was a strange and turbulent time for our Black cousins to the south. The civil rights movement was in full swing, and while we Canadians were appalled at the treatment of American Blacks, there were many among us here at home who held the same negative feelings towards those of us who were Black living in Canada. That's not to say that we didn't have many friends who were not Black, and I mean true friends that stood with you against adversity and spoke up when they felt we as Blacks were being treated unfairly. Those friends helped to make some of the happiest memories of our teenage years.

In some ways, Harry and I felt it was strange being seen as different while believing that we were no different than the white students we went to school with. Most of the emphasis on the difference was placed there by teachers and the parents of the kids we met each day in the hallways of North Vancouver High School. Most parents' negative attitudes emerged if you developed a friendship with their daughters. You knew instantly that all the stereotypical knowledge they had about Blacks, and in particular Black males, rushed forward and was applied to you. It wasn't too difficult to tell the difference between those who saw us as teenage boys with raging hormones and those who saw us as Black. Very few of the parents whose daughters we showed an interest in were colour-blind when they saw us.

Despite the social attitudes of the day, much of the enjoyment in Harry's teenage years was the result of his athletic ability and the successes he had playing baseball, football, rugby and hockey and competing in track and field. Harry had the focus and dedication to training that made him above average in the sports he played. It is that focus and dedication that took him to the heights he achieved in the track world.

When Harry burst onto the scene as one of the world's greatest sprinters, he was not prepared to handle the public attention that was heaped on him, and this caused confusion. Harry was basically a shy person, and that shyness was often misinterpreted as aloofness. Coupled with his shyness was a desire to protect his privacy, and this combination caused some people to believe that he was unfriendly when he wouldn't reveal personal details.

While reading this book, I was reminded of the many intimate moments Harry and I shared as Black youth and young adults discussing our feelings, hopes and plans for the future. It was great having a person my own age living in the same circumstances as myself, sharing the same experiences. It was this kind of relationship that helped us keep our sanity intact. We used to joke about what we called "racial schizophrenia," which we interpreted as living in a white environment and being Black. For certain, Harry's "Blackness" had to be suppressed a lot more than mine, because I had the advantage of growing up with a Black community around me in Toronto and Boston before I moved to North Vancouver. On the other hand, Harry grew up with a very limited Black community around him and subsequently lacked Black role models.

Harry and I were brought together at North Van High School by two things—our colour and our interest in sports. We played together on the school rugby team. Outside of school, we played baseball for a team sponsored by Fen Burdett. During the fall season, while Harry played football, I stuck to basketball, but we managed to socialize when the games and practices were done.

I recall the graduation dance in 1959 held at Brock Hall at the University of British Columbia and how much fun we had. It was a very heady time, a time that promised a great future. Harry was being wooed by American universities and offered athletic scholarships.

There was much to be hopeful about. If we only knew then how little time he did have, I wonder if he would have followed a different path.

I was one of the people who had lunch with Harry the day he died, and it was a great shock when only hours after we parted and agreed to meet two days later to have lunch again that I learned of his death. Of course, I didn't believe it was possible; although I knew he had not been well, it wasn't an illness I believed was life-threatening. I remember crying and feeling very sad, and at the same time, I was happy that Harry knew how I felt about him because I had told him that I loved him and was very proud of him and his accomplishments. I was happy, because too often, we never say those things to the people we love and only wish we had.

In *Running Uphill*, Fil Fraser has captured a side of Harry that others need to know, and he has done so in a way I'm not certain any other writer could have. The thorough research into the many aspects of Harry's life, including broken relationships, a dysfunctional family and the peaks and valleys of his athletic career as noted by the media, gives the reader an insight into one of Canada's greatest athletes and how these happenings shaped Harry's life. Had Harry had the great advantages of today's sprinters with unlimited time to practise and great sums of money available to them, I believe he could have set a world record for the 100 metres that they would still be trying to best. To this day, I am convinced that Harry's tremendous speed as a sprinter makes him the fastest runner of the past century. This book is a must-read, allowing us a peek into the private world of what it was like being a part of a Black family in Canada and capturing the exploits of a dedicated and talented Canadian who brought a great deal of pride to his country.

Foreword by Brian Pound[2]

Harry Jerome was the sum of many parts: great athlete, educator, sports official, champion of the underprivileged, husband and father, part radical, part activist, media target.

And he was my best friend, which, under the circumstances, went against the grain, when you consider that when we first met, I was part of the media circus that Harry would, a few years later, come to mistrust.

We first met in 1958, during the Vancouver and District High School Track and Field Eliminations, a five-day event to select athletes for the V and D finals at Empire Stadium. I was reportering for the *Vancouver Province*, and Harry was a sprinter representing North Vancouver High School. Harry went on to qualify for two sprint finals, winning one and finishing second in the other, tying with another sprinter for the overall Senior Boys title.

One year later, those elimination trials would become the "Harry Jerome Trials" as he dominated both the 100- and 220-yard qualifying races, and people were predicting he would break both meet records, held since 1928 by Vancouver's Percy Williams.

I remember calling Percy Williams a few days before the finals to ask him for his thoughts on Jerome possibly erasing both his records, to which Williams replied, "My god, do they both stand? I don't read the papers much."

Harry did the expected at that V and D meet, but he was able to break only one of Percy's marks, the 220 yards. He slipped coming out of the blocks and missed the 100-yard record by one-tenth of a second.

That, really, was the beginning of Harry Jerome's historic climb in the world of track and field.

Following the high school meet, I asked Harry if there was anything he would like to do to celebrate. He answered that he would like to meet Percy Williams. There has been a misconception out there that the two met for the first time at a reception. Not true. With the cooperation of Williams, I managed to get the two of them together for a meeting and photo shoot at a clothing store down the street from where Percy worked at an insurance company. The *Province* ran the photo just a few days after the high school meet.

They remained in touch off and on until Percy's untimely death.

I sit here remembering my dear friend who left us all too soon. I remember the many lunches we had that always ended up with us discussing what was wrong with the amateur sport system both in BC and nationally. I remember covering all those meets where Harry, with his amazing speed, dazzled the onlookers. I remember his injuries and his remarkable comeback. I remember his frustration with certain members of the media. I remember discussions about his personal life. I remember his fear about the headaches he was having and not knowing what was causing them. I remember getting that unexpected phone call telling me my friend had passed away, within an hour and a half of me saying goodbye to him as he climbed into a car to be taken to a friend's house. I remember an incredible individual who many said was bitter throughout his short life, but who in reality was nothing of the sort, an individual who really went out of his way to try and make things better for a whole lot of different people.

Harry Jerome was a sprinter. He ran fast with an incredible flowing motion, quite unlike any other sprinter of his era. Theirs was mainly power running. Harry's style was pure poetry.

A sprinter is a special athlete whose event is over in just seconds. By their very nature, sprinters tend to be moody at times and aloof. By his own admission, Harry was that at times, which may explain his often-stormy relationship with the media.

But it doesn't explain why many of them went out of their way to crucify him in print and on radio and TV.

When Harry returned from the Rome Olympics where many of the world media had labelled him a "quitter" for pulling up during his race, he sat down with me and told me he could have finished the race, but he would have had to crawl on his hands and knees to do it.

When he failed to finish at the British Empire and Commonwealth Games in Perth, the media were once again on his case. The follow-up operation, which almost finished his career, was ignored by many media members who had earlier criticized him.

I remember being at a track meet in New Westminster where Harry was approached by a sportscaster who wanted to do an interview for his 5:00 PM sportscast. Harry, who at the time was just minutes away from his race, said he'd be happy to do it after the race. The sportscaster didn't wait around and instead went back to his station and spent his entire sportscast telling the listeners what a spoiled brat Harry Jerome was.

Over the years, I was privy to many such incidents, and I told Harry to just ignore them. He was just too good an athlete to let it bother him. This conversation came during a national track and field championship in Ontario, and we sat up until 3:30 in the morning discussing things and drinking the odd bottle of beer. I left at 3:30 AM. Harry went out the next morning and equalled the meet record.

It has always baffled me how those who criticized Harry during those turbulent races in Rome and Perth came to praise him when he finally won his gold medal at the British Empire and Commonwealth Games in Jamaica in 1966 and his bronze medal in the 1964 Olympics in Tokyo.

And what a great moment it was for this writer to be there in Jamaica when Harry won that gold medal, finally silencing all those critics. Finally, after seven years of frustration and turmoil, climbing the podium of victory.

On the following pages, you will read the Harry Jerome story, beautifully written and researched by Fil Fraser, who unfortunately never met Harry. But Fil has carved out a book that will remain a testimony to one of Canada's greatest athletes.

And this writer is so proud to have played a small part in it.

Introduction

*I remembered the stories
that my mother and her
parents told me as a child,
the stories of a family trying
to explain itself.*

–Barack Obama

The stories in this book came to me from the family and friends, from the reporters and the fans who observed, or were part of, the too-short history of one of Canada's greatest athletes. No one of them, not even those closest to him, could fully explain his life—his drives, his character. Perhaps by setting down their recollections and by scouring the records, we can gain enough insight to begin to understand a complex, compelling life. I never met Harry Jerome, partly the result of living in a country that has too much geography, but also because Blacks who lived and worked in mainstream Canada in the days when "getting along" led to a lot of subtle, often unconscious, self-censorship, tended to stay away from each other. We lived in the white world and got used to, and sometimes even liked, being the only Black person in so many rooms.

Everything, of course, flows from context. Like the blind men examining the elephant, each observer gains a unique but very different view. The challenge of a biography is to bring together as many perspectives and to illuminate as many facets of the subject as possible. In the end, we will learn that Harry Jerome was as much a product of the Canada in which he lived as he was of his own inner drives and genetic inheritance.

Ever wonder why so many athletes and entertainers are Black? Why so many Chinese worked in restaurants and laundries? Why so many Jews went into buying and selling? Why the most innovative and successful new entrepreneurs often come from minority groups? Some argue that some ethnic groups have a special talent, even a genetic aptitude, for the fields they enter. In fact, recently reported studies have speculated on why so many Jews have won Nobel Prizes; why so many of the best runners are African or have African roots; why Chinese are more likely to be thin. For me, a more compelling case can be made for the fact that, for many but not all minorities, entry into "normal" mainstream professions and occupations was, and often still is, difficult or impossible. The walls barring acceptance could be, both then and now, hopelessly high, penetrable only just often enough to create "the exception that makes the rule" and allowing those who control the mainstream to comfort themselves with the illusion that all minorities, if they will only work hard enough, *can* make it. It's true that those who do make it work very hard—but many others work just as hard or harder and are denied.

A compelling illustration of the mainstream mindset, so much a part of the way things are that most people don't see it for what it is, can be found every Monday morning in the Report on Business section of "Canada's national newspaper," the *Toronto Globe and Mail*. Each week, the *Globe* runs pictures of appointees to high-level corporate positions. Week after week, the section, which can fill up to half a page or more, displays the faces of white, middle-aged men. There is a scattering of women, never close to challenging the majority; there is the occasional Chinese or South Asian face and, very occasionally— the exception to prove the rule—a Black one. What is clear is that in an era when corporate Canada rivals and often eclipses governments, at all levels in terms of power and influence, these are the corporate commanders who run the country with a single-minded dedication to the paramount interests of "shareholder value." Minorities make the list, rarely at the highest levels of power—just often enough to demonstrate that it is possible for them to break through. I once contemplated renting a billboard in downtown Toronto and displaying a typical *Globe* appointments page under the caption "Affirmative Action."

When no one will give you a job, you have to make your own— you do what you must do. In bygone days, Black men in the Americas boxed, sang, danced (Stepin Fetchit[3]) or toiled as janitors or porters, while their women, if they were respectable, walked or took the bus "uptown" to work as maids. Chinese, forced into entrepreneurship, started businesses in which they did what was considered to be women's work—laundry and cooking. Japanese took to fishing, and Ukrainians, sucked in by overly glorified images of the Canadian West, worked the land. Many Jews, such as the fathers of Canadian icons Harry Rosen and Joe Shoctor, started as junk dealers and learned to do business. I still remember the old Jew who rattled through the Catholic streets of East End Montréal every week in a rickety, horse-drawn wagon, calling out "Rags, rags."

Most immigrants who managed to get into Canada scratched out a living in occupations often distant from their original training or education—jobs that mainstream workers did not care to do. The greater truth about the predisposition of minorities towards certain occupations may be that, after generations of inequity, the need to survive led to the evolution of adaptive traits and abilities. But the scientific jury on that subject will be out for a long while yet. Meanwhile, it is self-evident that the playing field remains far from level, and that the most enduring handicaps to equality are based on race and religion.

Brandeis Denham Jolly came to Canada from Jamaica in 1955, well ahead of the larger waves of immigration from the Caribbean islands and elsewhere that have changed Toronto into one of the most multicultural communities in the world. The waves followed Prime Minister John Diefenbaker's early-1960s overhaul of the immigration laws that had restricted immigrants to residents of a list of selected European countries and the old, white British Commonwealth, to allow new Canadians to qualify for admittance on the basis of skills and education, rather than on race, religion or country of origin. Few Canadians today recognize that it was the radical Diefenbaker who initiated the changes in immigration law that changed the face of the country.

After earning a Bachelor of Science degree from Montréal's McGill University, Jolly taught in the Ontario public school system, first in rural areas and then, specializing in chemistry and physics, at Forest Hill Collegiate in a tony Toronto neighbourhood. He worked on a study of air pollution for Metropolitan Toronto and did nutrition research for the Government of Jamaica. Jolly had an extraordinary talent for entrepreneurship that led to successful ownership of a variety of real estate properties and businesses, including the Tyndall Estates Retirement Home in Mississauga.

Early on, he involved himself in minority and human rights issues, becoming the publisher of *Contrast*, a community newspaper that championed equality for the city's growing Black population. Jolly is the founder and CEO of Toronto's first urban music radio station, Flow 93.5, and a partner in a sister radio station, The Bounce, in Edmonton, Alberta. Both stations have changed the auditory landscape in their respective markets, actively creating new stars and reflecting the musical tastes of a demographic that had not been on the radar of mainstream broadcasters. Even though hip problems have affected his mobility, Jolly, once a competitive tennis player, today projects a fashionably dressed image of power and authority.

On October 21, 1982, Denham Jolly gathered some 25 business leaders in a Toronto restaurant, aptly named the Underground Railroad. He wanted to create a movement that would recognize achievement and create role models for young men and women—young Black men and women—who faced high barriers to success in the mainstream world. That evening, the Black Business and Professional Association (BBPA) and the idea for an annual Black Achievement Awards ceremony came into being. Like many ethnically based movements, it became essential to its community, demonstrating to Black Canadians, young and old, that they *could* succeed, and that through hard work and perseverance, barriers could be made to fall in the wake of the ground-breaking efforts of the extraordinary women and men whose achievements the BBPA would celebrate.

It was fitting that Jolly and his colleagues would invite one of Canada's most extraordinary athletes, Black or white, to be the keynote speaker at the first Achievement Awards to be held the following spring. Harry Winston Jerome was Canada's fastest man, a sports icon—the first man to simultaneously hold world records for both the 100-yard and 100-metre sprints.[4] He represented Canada in three

Olympics and twice in each of the British Empire and Commonwealth Games and the Pan American Games, picking up scores of medals at other national and international track meets along the way. At the age of 42, as he prepared to share his experiences at the first Black Achievement Awards, Harry had matured into a respected teacher and an advocate for athletic youth development. After a challenging life in athletics, he was now beginning to take firm stands in the promotion of racial equality.

But less than two months after that Toronto meeting, Harry Jerome was dead. Doctors were unable to clearly diagnose the cause of the brain seizure that led to his passing on the afternoon of December 7, 1982. The BBPA, on the suggestion of Black broadcaster Hamlin Grange, named the Achievement Awards for him, and since the first presentations on March 5, 1983, the Harry Jerome Awards have been held annually in Toronto. The black tie affair, usually held in the Toronto Convention Centre, has attracted five or six hundred attendees, including politicians from prime ministers to members of local municipal councils and often the Governor General. Up to 2000 are expected to attend the 2007 event, the 25th anniversary of Harry's Death.

Many remember Harry Jerome, often vaguely, as Canada's, and one of the world's, fastest men through much of the 1960s. But there is a dark shadow to the memory. Prior to the 1960 Rome Olympics, the sports establishment built Harry Jerome up into a national symbol, virtually awarding him the gold medal before the race was run. When an injury in the final pre-race heat forced him to withdraw, national sportswriters were sorely disappointed, some demonstrably outraged that their prophecy had not come true. They branded Jerome as a quitter, saying that he didn't have the "stuff" to compete under the pressure of the big races. One of them reported, erroneously, that there had been no injury. The writers were even more hostile after he suffered a severe, career-threatening injury at the 1962 British Empire and Commonwealth Games in Perth, Australia. Jerome paid heavy dues, and his vilification by the mainstream sports press of the day is an unlovely example of Canadian journalistic history that will be fully explored in this book.

To members of Canada's Black community, Harry Jerome is an unblemished hero—one of its greatest role models. I, proudly, won a Harry Jerome Award in 1999 for "excellence in the professions." I was, at the time, president and CEO of Vision TV, a national television channel. With the award, my awareness of Jerome and his accomplishments came into sharper focus. But I didn't really begin to know the man until Denham Jolly suggested I write his biography.

I discovered, and then was touched by, a great deal of resonance between Jerome's life and my own, and even more between his life and that of my late brother Frank, who, in an overlapping era, was a successful halfback in the Canadian Football League (CFL). Both Frank and Harry excelled in several sports, including hockey and baseball; both had acquired good educations and career-building experience through sports scholarships at American universities. Frank was a star player in the Québec Junior Hockey League, but when it became clear that there would be no place for him in the NHL, he opted for a career in football. Jerome, according to his coaches and friends, could have achieved star status in either hockey, which he continued to play as an amateur through most of his adult life, or in baseball. He declined lucrative offers from both the BC Lions and the Calgary Stampeders football clubs.

But perhaps the deepest point of resonance between us was the experience of being part of a Black household whose parents chose to raise their families in the Canadian mainstream, rather than to live in the (in some ways) more comfortable ethnic communities into which they might have settled. Those of us raised in white communities used to feel a certain amount of envy towards those of our race who lived in the seemingly warm, though clearly disadvantaged, Black neighbourhoods, where shared experience created a sense of togetherness that could be both an anchor and a shield. On the other hand, some who grew up in what were often near-ghettoes have reported that making the transition to life in the wider society often was and continues to be painfully difficult. Those of us stuck in the mainstream had little choice but to take our lumps and try to learn to survive and succeed. Adapting to the mainstream means living in the mainstream. Your friends, your classmates, your fellow workers, the people you socialize with, the people you date and marry are likely to be white. While that never means that you forget who you are—the world won't let you do that—your lifestyle can create barriers of misunderstanding and suspicion between you and those who live "in the community." This dichotomy was clearly a factor in the life of Harry Jerome and his family, and in my own.

Until the relatively recent past, Canadians who belonged to ethnic minorities faced challenges vastly different—both for better and for worse—from those confronted by today's generation. Up until the passing, in 1982, of the Canadian Charter of Rights and Freedoms, Canada was still (in spite of Book IV of the 1963 Royal Commission on Bilingualism and Biculturalism, which examined the "Cultural Contribution of the Other Ethnic Groups") a "white *man's* country." Many clubs, hotels, restaurants, universities and other facilities were still, sometimes unofficially, sometimes blatantly and publicly, off limits to minorities ranging from "coloured" people to people from the "wrong" European countries and to Jews, no matter where they came from.

Our Canadian barriers were more subtle than those south of the border, but the result was just as harsh; in some ways more so, because the image our country projected, an image in which so many of us tried so hard to believe, was of an open, egalitarian, non-racist society. In the United States, discrimination was usually open and often legally sanctioned; you knew exactly where you stood. In Canada, though a few establishments displayed signs that said "No Dogs or Jews," people rarely told you outright that you were not wanted. Your job application would be graciously accepted, but you would never get a call back; apartment buildings advertising vacancies were suddenly fully rented when you showed your face or revealed your name. In one study, researchers wrote seeking reservations from exclusive resorts. When they used Anglo-Saxon names, acceptance was almost automatic. But when the requests came from individuals with "foreign-sounding" names, "No Vacancy" signs popped up almost everywhere. In a modern echo, the *Globe and Mail* Careers section reported on August 2, 2006, how a man named Ravi Prashad sent job applications to five prospective employers using his own name and five more to the same firms using the name Roger Pritchard. Aside from the name change, the applications were identical. Roger Pritchard got three responses; Ravi Prashad got none. The story also noted a study carried out by the *American Economic Review* under the title "Are Emily and Greg More Employable than Lakisha and Jamal?" The conclusion: applications with "white" names received 50 percent more calls for interviews than those with "African American" names, though each application showed equivalent qualifications.

You could go into a restaurant that gave no sign that you weren't welcome, until, after waiting for an agonizingly long time, you realized that no server would come to your table. Newspaper stories of Black celebrities who were unwelcome in first-class hotels made you wary of where you went—at the height of her career in the 1950s, Eartha Kitt was refused accommodation at Montréal's Ritz-Carlton Hotel. In upscale stores, clerks would follow you around to make sure you didn't steal anything; they would avoid talking to you, unless it was to confront you with the chilling "Can I help you?"

Well into the 1980s, people of colour had to develop adaptive skills different from those required by today's generation of rapidly growing minority populations. The tipping point was the passage of the Charter and the legislation and regulations that have evolved from it. Until the Charter, fair employment, fair accommodation and general human rights laws, where they existed, had few useful tools for enforcement. But for more than a generation, the Charter, firmly embedded in Canada's constitution, has created higher levels of protection through increasingly effective anti-discrimination laws and institutions. And, through education and example, enforcement of the laws has resulted in an increasingly enlightened public. But even today, as the bull's eye of discrimination shifts to Muslim and Middle Eastern groups, all minorities still need a Swiss-army-knife, ready-for-anything intellectual, and particularly emotional, survival kit: a thick skin to walk away from barriers you know are, at least in the short term, insurmountable; a quick wit to talk your way out of situations when you are cornered; fast feet to run when you have to; fast fists for when you cannot, or will not run; the fortitude to challenge discrimination when you can; and above all, *above all*, to counter the self-sabotaging sense of inferiority that too often lurks hidden in the deepest corners of your being, an unshakable belief in your own value as a human being.

Harry Jerome died the year that the Canadian Charter of Rights and Freedoms came into being. Without its protection, he developed a unique and powerful mental and emotional tool kit to help him overcome the unavoidable adversities of his time. Its central tool was an extraordinarily powerful sense of discipline, a spartan practice of keeping his troubles to himself and a near-superhuman work ethic. Had he lived longer, there is little doubt that he would have made an even more significant contribution to his country than he was able to achieve as an athlete and would have been recognized and celebrated along with the likes of Oscar Peterson, Lincoln Alexander and Austin Clarke and, yes, Donovan Bailey, Daniel Igala and Jarome Iginla.

Among the realities that have made writing this biography at once easy and difficult is the fact that many of Harry's contemporaries are still alive, their memories still sharp. I have spoken at length with his running mates, his coach, his one-time manager, many of his friends, his sisters, at least one of his girlfriends, his ex-wife, his daughter and his mother, who in the spring of 2005 was alive and feisty at the age of 85. As well, I spoke with some of the journalists who covered his career. Many of the insights I gained and many of the stories you'll read throughout this volume are filtered through their memories.

Others come from an exhaustive study of the extensive newspaper coverage that both lauded and denounced him throughout most of his career. Harry's public legend was an invention of the sports media, often unfriendly and not infrequently vicious in its coverage of his triumphs and his failures.

I hope that I have been able to maintain enough distance from my subject to be reasonably objective. At the same time, I believe that it's only fair, as I set the stage for the chapters that follow, that I give you, the reader, some appreciation of the baggage that I bring to this work. What experiences, what biases tint the lenses through which I see Harry Jerome? Race and, in some ways, family circumstances give me a deep understanding of the challenges he faced; my family, like his, was not a perfect model for life. But you also need to know that I am not at all like Harry Jerome. As a youngster, I decidedly did *not* want a career in sports or entertainment—roles I thought would just make me part of the "Negro" stereotype, even though as a teenager I was a pretty fast runner (I had to be—I wasn't much of a fighter) and could play a mean boogie-woogie on the piano. I refused to eat watermelon. I shuddered at the idea of straightening my hair, even though for years my father wore a "stocking cap" made of one of my mother's old nylons, to smooth down his hair. For years, to the later profit of a number of dentists, I rejected the notion that I should have "pearly white teeth" (like Louis Armstrong) and failed to brush as I should have.

As a careful boy growing up in East End Montréal, I was shy, confused and thought for a long time that God had put me on the wrong planet. Night after night, as a preadolescent, I prayed that he would take me back and correct his mistake. The *Globe and Mail*'s Roy Macgregor once quoted me as saying, "Don't ask me to explain my life; I'm an oddity even to myself." But if you google me, you'll see that I have been blessed with a long career as a broadcaster, journalist, movie producer, teacher and author—things I could only dream of as a teenager. There were no Black broadcasters in Canada when I went to work for Foster Hewitt's Toronto radio station in 1951; my role models were white. I was spellbound by radio, possibly because part of my (surely unconscious) thinking at the time was built around the notion that, over the airwaves, if you sounded white, people would forget that you were Black. But I didn't really understand that until I figured it out much, much later. I stayed away from TV until the late 1960s because I thought that, unless I was an entertainer or an athlete, I would not be welcome.

I came into broadcasting at a fortuitous time. Blacks in Canada were not numerous and were certainly no threat to anyone. They were mostly compliant—maids and minstrels, sweepers and porters— significantly different from the case in today's Toronto, where "visible minorities" are on the cusp of becoming the majority. In the 1950s mainstream, Canadians could afford to be "nice" to selected minorities, often seeing their goodwill as a demonstration ("some of my best friends," etc.) of their generous spirits. It could be argued that treating selected minorities well was almost a psychic necessity, as awareness of the shocking treatment of Japanese, Jewish, German, Ukrainian and Italian Canadian citizens during the world wars began to bubble into the national consciousness. It was quite different from the 21st-century experience, where, in the big cities, but more particularly in many parts of rural Canada, many whites fearfully, defensively and sometimes aggressively, try to defend their "way of life."

"We didn't vote to change the immigration law. Who the hell decided to let all of these people in?"[5] one of them asked me as I toured the country as a member of the so-called "Spicer Commission."[6]

But even though, in preadolescence, I had, on many occasions, to either fight my way home from school or outrun my adversaries, I have faced few racially based personal threats during my adult life. And I have had little trouble coping with those that crossed my path. In Regina, where, in the early 1960s, an apartment owner refused to rent to me on racial grounds, I was the first to invoke the Saskatchewan Fair Practices Accommodations Act. I turned down their offer of an apartment after they lost the case.

All my life I have lived and worked contentedly in the mainstream, and I count my blessings. That is not to say, however, that I have been unaware of the challenges faced by others of my race. Not everyone had the survival skills that my siblings and I developed growing up in a white, sometimes hostile, mostly French Canadian, semi-rural community on the east end of the island of Montréal. I once wrote that I thought that *maudit negre*[7] was one word. I have faced enough racism to understand the pain of those whose life journey has not been as easy as mine. My younger brother, the late Francis Malcolm "Frank" Fraser, faced much tougher challenges, both as a student at a Tennessee State A&I University during the racially explosive 1950s, and through a nearly decade-long career in the CFL. Some of his coaches, brought in from the American South, were self-righteously blatant in their racism.

So, as I approach the life of Harry Jerome, I bring a personal empathy to the challenges he faced, a deep understanding of the prejudice and discrimination that seared his life. As I reflect on the realities of being Black in Canada, some recent reading has had a profound influence on my thinking and, in some ways, on the shaping of this book. This is not just a sports story. Barack Obama's bestseller, *Dreams from My Father,* has opened up levels of self-understanding that I had failed to fully grasp throughout an already long lifetime. Obama is the son of a Black father and a white mother. Since his dramatic speech to the 1998 Democratic national convention, he has become a rising star in American politics. Early in 2007, he declared his intention to run for the presidency of the United States. People are saying that if the U.S. ever elects a Black president, it will be him.

His biography, written with tear-welling power, is an important read for any child of mixed race—more so for anyone who is Black. As so many know deep in their bones, whatever your racial mix, if any part of it is Black and it shows, then Black is how the world sees and treats you. And, for reasons that are not the subject of this book, Africans, both at home and in the diaspora, are too often seen to be at the bottom of the racial totem pole. I began to absorb Barack's "smack-upside-the-head" lessons as, on a cross-Canada flight to a Toronto board meeting, the stunningly insightful, powerfully literate pages of *Dreams from My Father* tore at my heart. Obama throws blinding light on why so many of us have distorted relationships with our fathers, who we struggle to understand and accept, and who faced even greater challenges than we. Obama lights up dark corners of our spirit, revealing how we are so often blindsided by our own racism, so deeply internalized that we don't even know it's there. He dissects, almost surgically, some of the toughest internal battles faced by Black men.

But this book is about Harry Winston Jerome. His story is, inevitably, also about the Canada he experienced, as much about the times in which he lived as about him. But Jerome is the centrepiece. I wondered why no one had written this book long ago. Journalist Brian Pound expressed an interest and talked to Jerome about it; they even agreed on a title: *Run Angry, Run Fast*. "His upbringing had not been ideal, and he once told me that the only way he could get rid of his anger was to run," Pound related.

I found a carbon copy of a letter, dated May 8, 1968, from Dorothy Hanson, a member of the editorial department of Macmillan Publishers, which turned down a proposal from a Mr. Greenburg, of Toronto, for a book on Jerome. She wrote that she was not convinced that there was a market for a book based solely on Harry Jerome's life. She encouraged a larger work—the story of Canadian track and field "with particular emphasis on the careers of Carruthers, Kidd and Jerome." North Vancouver journalist Len Corben also considered a biography.

Potential biographers may have been put off by Harry's sister, Valerie Parker, who has herself written a book, which, after many years, has failed to find a publisher. She was the only member of the Jerome family who refused to cooperate with me, claiming that I would "undermine" her own chances for publication. As the member of the family purportedly closest to Harry, and as a once promising athlete herself, she would have been the first person that any potential biographer would have approached. I am sorry that I was unable to win her trust.

And so I come to the challenge of telling a very Canadian story whose echoes have universal relevance. I hope to reveal a man who was, without question, larger than life. He may be relatively well remembered as the elite athlete he was. But he is still in many ways an enigma even to those who celebrate his achievements. Few know much about the turmoil of his personal life, his unrelenting crusading spirit and the challenging path he was travelling when death came too soon. He was a man of immense courage and determination. But he was a man subject to the influences of his family heritage and of the country he lived in.

In the short arc of his life, Harry Jerome lit the way for new generations of Canadians.

Chapter One

Remembering Harry

*Each of us chose a costume, an armour
against uncertainty. At least on the basketball
court, I could find a community of sorts,
with an inner life all its own. It was there that I would
make my closest white friends, on turf where blackness
couldn't be a disadvantage.*

—Barack Obama

On February 8, 2005, Paul Winn gathered a small group of Harry Jerome's close friends for an evening of storytelling and reminiscing. It was a great opportunity for me to connect with people who had worked and played with Jerome—people who, in many ways, knew more about him than anyone. The event took place on a dark, rainy evening at the Richmond, BC, home of Konrad and Violet Tittler. The group, beside the Tittlers, included Harry's long-time coach John Minichiello, Dr. Auby (Al) Rader, a dentist and former University of Alberta athlete Lou Mohan, with whom Jerome had coached kids' soccer after he retired from track, and Paul Winn.

The stories told that evening gave me insights into the character of Harry Jerome that I would have found difficult to glean in any other way. Al Rader remembered an incident that illustrated how Harry would get his friends involved in his training. He had been at the Rader's home for dinner. (Others around the room cheerfully chipped in with stories of how Harry always had a habit of dropping in on his friends around dinnertime.)

"There was always a place for him at the table," Rader said. "And he was always very respectful. For all the time we knew him, he always called my wife Mrs. Rader. He never used her first name."

After dinner, Harry said, "What are you doing, Doc, for the rest of the evening? Have you got an hour?" Rader protested that he had a big day ahead and planned to go to bed early. But Harry insisted they go over to the local school, which had a cinder track. "It was raining cats and dogs," Rader said. "But I take my starting pistol and my stopwatch…and he does starts, running 20 metres or so, over and over… We did that for an hour. I wasn't his coach. He just said, 'This is what we're going to do.'"

Rader was a coach in his own right, then a high-level member of the Olympic movement in Vancouver. "Harry's the only top-notch

Harry in Perth, Australia, just before attempting the 100-yard dash in the British Empire Games.

world athlete I've ever met who was modest about his accomplish-ments. ....And I never met anybody who looked after his friends the way he did."

One story, as much as anything else, illustrates the kind of contri-bution Harry would have made to young athletes had his life been extended. It came from John Minichiello, his coach since high school days, when they began a lifelong relationship that continued after Harry retired from competition, when both men added a new dimen-sion to their relationship built around coaching youngsters.

"He was a great motivator," Minichiello related. "One year, we coached a soccer club in Richmond. Someone in the Richmond Soc-cer Association came up with the brilliant idea that boys are most troublesome when they're 14 or 15. All of the teams in Richmond had one or two troublesome 14- or 15-year olds—it was the beginning of getting into drugs and other problems. They came up with the idea that if they put all of these kids on one team, somehow that would clean up the league and take care of the kids. It was almost like incar-cerating them on one team.

"So, Harry and I took on these kids—a few of them had tried to steal a car or two. Basically they were troubled kids, for all sorts of reasons, some not of their own making. Some were okay athletes, some were not. We started out losing games, but there was Harry pre-suming all along that they were going to win. We'd practise, and all he talked about was 'You gotta believe you're going to win. Last Saturday we lost 5–1, next Saturday we're going to win.' Well, at the end of the year, we ended up in the finals for the provincial competition against a powerhouse team. Harry spoke to the kids. There were no great speeches—it was just one on one or with little groups, and at the end of the practice, he's saying, 'You guys are becoming somebody...You are becoming somebody.' And, sure enough, the week before the game, he said, 'This is it. You're going to show everybody.' Because these kids knew that they had been rejected. They were rejects from the league.

We went out there, and that game was a 1–0 game. That team, in the early part of the season, would have beaten these boys by 10 or 11 goals—and it ended up they had to hang on to win 1–0.

"The kids walked off the field—and they were all winners. 'We showed them,' they crowed. 'They were lucky.' It was a fascinating thing to watch, because it happened so easily. Harry had it in his own mind that there is something [in you] about winning, and you either recognized it and knew what it was all about, or you didn't. And, slowly, he was putting this into the heads of these young, tough kids. When Harry spoke, they paid attention, because this was Harry Jerome. The kids always said, 'Let's have a race.' They wanted to race with Harry, of course…and their eyes practically popped out of their heads. He was only at half or three-quarter speed by the time he reached the 50-yard line, but they were 10 to 20 yards behind him. They got a concept of excellence. That's what I kept seeing."

Harry's other long-time coach, Bill Bowerman, in an August 3, 1964, letter to the Board of Governors of Simon Fraser University, echoed Minichiello's appreciation of Harry's coaching and leadership skills. Jerome had applied for a teaching position at Simon Fraser. Bowerman wrote:

> I recommend him to you with my highest com-
> pliments and without reservation.
>
> In the course of his athletic competition and
> pursuit of an education, he has overcome not only
> a muscle injury of catastrophic proportions, but also
> the psychological problems that an unfriendly and
> not-understanding press heaped upon him. He has
> gone about overcoming the injury and his quiet rela-
> tionship with the public in such a manner that he
> has again achieved a national championship and has
> placed himself among the top in his event in the
> world.

Harry Jerome in a race at a varsity track meet held at Hayward Field, Eugene, Oregon. He ran the 440 in 48.1 seconds. His relaxed running style made his speed seem almost effortless.

Probably the thing you will be most interested
in is the type of leadership that he has exercised during his educational pursuits at the University of Oregon. As an unpaid assistant, he has worked with our
freshman track men. His skill and leadership have
contributed materially to such achievements as a
world-record 440 relay team and two national championship teams.

Simon Fraser, in its wisdom, did not hire him. Achievement in
sports was not high on the agenda of Canadian universities.

Lou Mohan talked about how he had talked Harry into being
a member of the board of the Killarney Community Centre. They were
coaching a soccer team made up of kids from group homes, and one
youngster showed up without soccer shoes. "So Harry took off his
shoes and gave them to the kid. He never thought anything of it."

Others told stories of Harry calling up sports companies, most
often Adidas, and persuading them to provide shoes and other equipment, which he would give to the kids. Adidas became something
of a sponsor to Harry. A July 1964 note from Dick Bank, then the
Adidas U.S. factory representative, told Harry that he was air freight-
ing enough size 9.9 shoes to last him through the summer, and that,
furthermore, there would be new shoes in Tokyo (at the Olympics)—
"a new, still-lighter model with interchangeable spikes." That was
about as much support as Harry ever got from companies that today
lavish millions in endorsement fees on athletes.

The soccer field that Jerome and Mohan's kids played on would
have been greatly improved if it had lights. "He came in one day and
said, 'I got the lights.' 'What lights?' Mohan asked. 'I got the money
for the lights.'"

Jerome had approached Jerry Strongman and Stephen Rogers,
members of the BC Legislature, and had persuaded them to find a quarter of a million dollars to improve the playing field. "And those lights—
at 49th and Kerr—are there today," Mohan said with some pride.

Harry phoned dentist Al Rader one day, asking, "What are you doing Thursday at noon?" "I'll be working, what do you think I'll be doing?" Rader replied. But Harry said, "I want you to come with me. I'm going to the Lions Club. They are going to give us money for some equipment for the schools. I want you to talk to them. You come with me and tell them what I need." Rader protested but did what Harry asked of him, and the Lions Club came through.

"He used his power in a good way," said Violet Tittler. "And he was a good friend. He kept his friends close and took them with him through his life." She had met Harry on the track, when she was a runner. She came home and told her husband, Konrad, "Guess who I trained with today? And, you know, he plays hockey, and I told him that you really love to play hockey." "This is Friday night at dinnertime," Konrad interjected. "Seven o'clock, the phone rings…'Hi, it's Harry. Wanna play hockey tonight?'" So they met, for the first time, at nine o'clock that evening on a neighbourhood rink in Richmond. "He loved to play hockey, and he would have been a very good hockey player had he chosen that.[8] We played together the whole season in a semi-industrial league." Tittler, a successful businessman, often travelled to events such as the Jamaica British Empire and Commonwealth Games with Jerome.

There is no doubt that the lives of the people who gathered in Richmond that evening were deeply affected by their friendship with Jerome. Here they were, more than two decades after his death, reminiscing, almost as if it were yesterday, about the impact he had on their lives. They travelled with him, put him up in their homes, worked and played with him and went out of their way to help him in any way they could. If he had lived, they said, he might well have gone into politics—"and we'd all be out there working for him." He had been approached to run by both the BC Social Credit and New Democratic parties. A cynic might say that these people were just attracted by his celebrity. But I came away from that evening convinced that they truly loved the man.

Harry Jerome didn't like living alone. He lived with the Tittlers for the better part of a year, sharing the basement with one of their sons. They day he died, he was on his way to spend a few days at the home of Jerry and Judy Strongman. Aside from the time he was married, and through a couple of other romantic live-in relationships, he roomed with his friends. Paul Winn, before and after both had married and divorced, was his most frequent apartment mate. They probably shared accommodation, off and on, for as many as five years between the time they left high school and Harry's passing. They could have been models for an *Odd Couple* television series. Harry was quiet, serious and self-contained. Paul, open, gregarious and fun-loving, was a classic model of what-you-see-is-what-you-get.

Towards the end of the evening, I asked those at the gathering to tell me their "best" stories about Harry. What memories stuck most poignantly in their minds? Without any prompting, for the first time in the evening, stories of racism came to the surface.

Al Rader: "The only time in my life I ever ran into prejudice was with Harry. We were on our way to an event in Spokane and stopped at a motel to get lodging for the night. We walked into the place, and the fellow said, 'We don't have any rooms.' And I said, 'Don't give me that, all the keys are still up there on the board.' He said, 'I told you, *we don't have any rooms.*' Harry grabbed me by the arm and said, 'Come on Doc, it's me.' And I didn't know what the hell he was talking about. I had no idea."

Paul Winn: "There was lots of prejudice around in North Vancouver, but Harry would never express it. During his first year at Oregon, he went into a frat house with a fellow athlete, Jim Pucket. Harry thought the place was quite nice. 'I'd like to stay here next term,' he said. 'You can't stay here.' 'Why not?' Harry asked, genuinely surprised. Pucket looked at him in amazement, 'You're Black.'"

"That really affected him," John Minichiello added. "He wrote me a letter about it."

The fact that racism was an unrelenting undercurrent in Jerome's life was just a fact of life for Blacks and many members of other racial and social minorities in the 1960s and 1970s. Individuals and groups responded with everything from outrage and violence (sometimes self-directed) to outright denial. Harry dealt with it by keeping a stoic rein on his emotions. Journalist Brian Pound told me that in Oregon, because he was a track star, Harry would sometimes break through the taboos. On one occasion, Pound was meeting him in a Eugene restaurant. A Black man came in and was told that he could not be served. But when Harry came in it was "Hey Harry, how are you?" Pound, who was a principal of the BC Sports Hall of Fame, is now on the Burnaby Parks and Recreation Board, in the Burnaby Hall of Fame and, in semi-retirement, is involved in supporting wheelchair athletics.

"I started coaching him when he was in grade 11," John Minichiello summed up. "You could see he was confident, shy and moody. But he was also kind to his friends. He was a straightforward person. He appeared to be controversial, but when you talked to him at length, you usually found out what motivated him. You can't compete at that level without having some anger and determination in you."

Chapter Two

Roots

Blacks are there but not there,
Like Sam the piano player or
Beulah the maid
or Amos and Andy on the radio
—shadowy, silent presences that
elicit neither passion nor fear.

–Barack Obama

It's difficult to precisely describe the ideal physique for a runner. Athletes such Percy Williams, Harry Jerome and Donovan Bailey, Canada's three great champions of the sprint, had distinctly different body types and running styles. Williams was small and slight; Bailey is large and muscular. But Jerome came as close as any to the image of the ideal runner. He was of average height, more lithe than muscular, his thighs displaying a physical predisposition for running. Journalist Brian Pound recalled, "He had the most fluid running style of any sprinter." Jerome's sports-savvy wife, Wendy, described him as "physically a very lovely specimen." There are different estimates of his height—his strong presence made him seem larger to observers (some reported him at 183 centimetres or more) than his actual 180-centimetre (5'11") stature.[9] All of these elements are captured in a beautiful, graceful statue of him in Vancouver's Stanley Park, created by Jack Harman, the sculptor who also built the statue of the 1954 "Miracle Mile" runners John Landy and Roger Bannister, which stands at the entrance to Vancouver's Empire Stadium.

If genetics play a role in determining what we become, Harry Jerome was destined to be a runner long before he was born. It's possible that even a tendency to injury was somehow part of his genetic makeup. His maternal grandfather, John Armstrong (Armie) Howard, born in St. Paul, Minnesota, in 1887, was a striking, 190-centimetre-tall athlete. He represented Canada in the 100- and 200-metre sprints at the 1912 Stockholm and the 1920 Antwerp Olympics but finished out of the medals. In Antwerp, perhaps prophetically, he pulled up lame.

"On the track, he suffered from muscle spasms when he overreached himself, just the way our grandson, Harry Jerome does now," Howard's wife, the late Edith Sumpton, told a reporter during an interview following the 1962 British Empire Games. "I remember in England, in 1919, it happened to Armie and again in Antwerp at the

Harry Jerome Sr. and Jr. at their home in North Vancouver.

Olympic Games of 1920, when he lost the 100 metres to the American, Charlie Paddock."

Armie and Edith met in England. Born in Chiswick, she was the very English daughter of a family of market gardeners that she said had, for generations, supplied flowers to Covent Gardens. Like many of her class, she patriotically joined the Women's Land Army during

World War I. And like thousands of other English girls in both world wars, she became a "war bride," swept away to a new life in the New World. Armie was a Red Cross bearer, serving with the Royal Canadian Medical Corps, a "coloured man" who had moved north in 1910, attracted by the lure of Canadian citizenship and life in a gentler land. They were married in London in 1919 and were soon blessed with a daughter, Elsie, who would become the mother of Harry Jerome. After the war, Armie decided to bring his bride and their new baby "home" to his adopted country. There are interesting but slightly differing accounts of their early life in Manitoba contained in features published more than a decade and a half apart by writers at *Victoria Colonist Magazine* on February 3, 1963, and July 22, 1979.

We know that the couple arrived in Winnipeg in the summer of 1920. Howard had represented Canada in the Olympics earlier that year, but "it was impossible for Armie to find work with so many returned men looking for work, so we headed for the farming community of St. Rose de Lac," Edith told a reporter. "In that area, we found very few people understood a mixed marriage, so we decided to go and live among the Indians, who we felt would have no racial prejudice." With help from the local Cree community, Armie built a 5.5-by-6-metre log cabin, which became their home for the next decade. The family homesteaded, broke up 10 acres of land and built up a small herd of cattle.

"The Indians taught us how to do many things," Edith remembered. "I learned to shoot and hunt and fish through a hole in the ice in the winter. I learned to hunt rabbits and sold them to a mink farmer (after we ate the hind legs), as well as how to catch weasels and lynx. Pretty soon I could skin an animal as fast as the Indians."

Three more children, all daughters, were born on the farm. In 1930, with Elsie turning 11, the family had to do something about schooling for the girls. Armie thought that they could home-school them. But Edith, a strong-willed woman, insisted they go to a real school in town. The disagreement led to a separation and an eventual divorce.

Edith and her daughters moved to Dauphin, where she worked as a cleaner in a medical facility and did housework to support her family. Armie Howard went to work as a sleeping car porter. He died unexpectedly of "double pneumonia" in 1937, at the age of 50. His passing, like that of his grandson, came too soon. And, like his grandson, in the end he had earned the respect of his community and was buried with full military honours. Oddly, it was 67 years later, in 2004, when he was belatedly inducted into the Manitoba Hall of Fame, which, on its 25th anniversary, decided to create a special Veteran Induction Ceremony, allowing past sports heroes to take their rightful place on the walls of the museum. The citation for "J. Army Howard," not entirely accurate, read:

> Born in Winnipeg, John Army Howard was a gifted natural athlete who ruled the Canadian sprint scene from 1912–15. As a member of Canada's Olympic team in 1912, he travelled overseas to Stockholm, Sweden, with fellow Hall-of-Famer Joe Keeper (inducted in 1984) as one of the premier sprinters at those games. In 1913, he dominated the Canadian Outdoor Championships held in Vancouver, winning gold in both the 100- and 220-yard dash events. A product of the Winnipeg North End Amateur Athletics Club (NEAAC), Howard enjoyed the prime of his career when Manitoba had many brilliant track athletes including Keeper and Laurie Armstrong (inducted in 1989).
>
> Howard joined the Canadian Expeditionary Force in 1917 and returned from the Great War in 1919. He worked for six years with the Canadian National Railway and ranched in the Riding Mountains starting in 1920. Army Howard's bloodlines were passed on to his grandson Harry Jerome, 1964 Olympic Bronze Medallist and a member of four halls of fame himself.

It was Harry Jerome's prowess that propelled his grandfather, who had long deserved to be there, into the Manitoba Hall of Fame.

Five years after Armie Howard's death, in 1942, Edith married Morris "Happy" Sumpton, a white man who also worked on the railway, but as a conductor—a position far superior, in status and in pay, to that of a sleeping car porter. His attitude towards the Black side of his extended family was redolent of the times. It was only after Sumpton's death and after Harry had gained international fame that Edith was moved to publicly express pride in both her first husband and her grandson. "He's just a second Armie Howard—his disposition, his moods—and tenderhearted just like his grandfather was. When he's running, he tries too hard. I saw this myself in Vancouver. When reporters say he's a quitter and comes from an unhappy family, they don't know what they're talking about. I'm not embittered, but my word, it makes me mad."

Edith Sumpton celebrated her 100th birthday on January 29, 1998. Her first daughter, Elsie, married Harry Jerome, who, like her father, also worked as a sleeping car porter. And, like her father, Harry Jerome Sr. started life as an American. Born in 1902, his family immigrated to Canada in 1910. When I met her in a Vancouver senior's residence, Elsie was, at 85, full of life and energy and in possession all of her faculties.

"Don't call me on Tuesdays," she said. "That's when I play bingo." She was bright-eyed and full of memories—too many of them painful. Women of her era, at the best of times, lived lives fraught with danger and systemic challenges. Her mixed racial heritage was not obvious—she looked vaguely southern European—but she was clearly proud of who she was, in all of its dimensions. She raged against the racism that had so coloured her life and that of her family. She had worked hard against great odds to keep them together, bringing her children up to be honest, productive citizens.

Until well into the 1960s, working on the railroad was the best job a Black man in Canada could get. It provided steady employment and,

in the circumstances, a pretty good wage. Sleeping car porters, especially during the Great Depression of the 1930s, were economically
better off than many white Canadians who had to scratch for the most
meagre subsistence. Thousands "rode the rails" in freight and cattle
cars, back and forth across the country in search of employment. Porters were the elite in the Black communities that grew up in railroad
centres such as Halifax, Montréal, Toronto, Winnipeg and Vancouver.
They played respected roles in church and community affairs, and
most saw to it that their children got a better education than had been
possible for them.

But, on the road, life was no picnic.

It was 1867, the year of Canada's birth, when the American Pullman Palace Car Company began the tradition of hiring Black men to
work exclusively as sleeping car porters, to "look after" white passengers in their rolling "hotels on wheels." The system was soon imported
into Canada and, like Harry Jerome Sr., many American Blacks
migrated to Canada to take up the jobs, for which, with a still small
Black population, there were not enough Canadian applicants. One
source[10] described the environment this way:

> Canadian railway companies avidly sought
> Black railroaders for sleeping car service because
> the image of broad-smiling, white-gloved, crisply
> uniformed black men provided a money-making
> triumph with Canada's wealthy railway clientele. . . .
> Once on the road, the sleeping car porter tended to his
> passengers' every whim. The porter greeted travellers,
> stowed luggage, pulled down berths in the evening
> and hurriedly converted them back into seats in the
> morning. Responsible for remembering passengers'
> schedules, he was severely reprimanded when some-
> one missed their stop. The porter, whom passengers
> condescendingly called "George" or "boy," served

Harry flanked by his sisters Valerie, left, and Caroline.

food, mixed drinks, shined shoes, cared for small
children, sick passengers and drunken ones, too.

Stanley G. Grizzle in his 1998 autobiography, *My Name's Not
George*, aptly describes life "on the road." Grizzle was one of the founders of the Brotherhood of Sleeping Car Porters in Canada, the grass-
roots union that fought to eventually improve the lot of Black porters.
"We had no identification to wear, and passengers often addressed us
as 'George,' after George Pullman," Grizzle wrote. "When they wanted
your attention, some would call you 'George.' This always got my back
up, and it irritated many other men as well. I would always correct
them by calmly saying, 'My name's not George.'" The book is a compelling chronicle of the struggles by Grizzle and his union compatri-
ots to achieve even the most rudimentary rights.

An award-winning National Film Board documentary, *The Road
Taken*, produced and directed by Selwyn Jacob, chronicles the life and

times of sleeping car porters. With a musical score written by Canadian composer and jazz pianist Joe Sealy, another son of a porter, the film examines the psychological millstone of serving passengers who might, on occasion, be respectful and kind, but who were more often rude and haughty. Porters worked under a demerit system in which the loss of "points" for talking back to passengers, for failing to do everything from emptying spittoons and shining shoes to making up beds according to iron-strict railroad standards, could lead to a suspension. Any problem involving money or women resulted in instant dismissal. Some of the younger porters fought off adventure-seeking white women. Some didn't. While porters, according to Nova Scotia historian, author, former porter and Order of Canada member Calvin Ruck, were the "elite of the Black community," they had no rights on the job. Porters were not allowed to apply for, let alone hold, any other occupation on the railroad—they were "non-persons."

"Endurance was the key," Ruck told Jacob. "If a man could endure, could be patient and courteous in a storm of abuse…his reward was vision.…It took tremendous strength to do this kind of work where racism was extreme."

One of the most heart-rending accounts of life on the road came from Ray Lewis, the first Black man to win Olympic medals for Canada. Looking strong and athletic, his fighting spirit evident even in his 80s, Lewis was born in Hamilton, Ontario, on October 8, 1910. He was featured in a television documentary series called *Hymn to Freedom*, produced by Almeta Speaks, which I had the honour to host and narrate.

In the program, Lewis talks about his athletic prowess as a schoolboy in his hometown of Hamilton, almost always in the face of the most overt racism. The school track coach didn't want him on his team, "but I could run so fast he had to put me on." When he was 15, a teacher, in front of the whole class, called him a "low-down dirty nigger, scum of the earth." With the same button-it-up spirit that later animated Harry Jerome, he did not tell his parents about the incident.

"My father would have said, 'Raymond, let's pray about it.' But I didn't want to pray, I wanted to kill the son of a bitch." He went, instead, to the principal, who did absolutely nothing about it. "These things made me angry," he told Almeta Speaks, "so every time the gun went off for the next 12 years, I raced against those two men. That's why I have a hundred medals."

Lewis had stacked up an impressive number of victories as a high school athlete but was rebuffed in his bid to represent Canada in the 1928 Olympics. Years later, he said, "I knew deep down why I was not selected. Prejudice in Canadian athletics played a big part in the decision." He was a bronze medallist in the 1932 Los Angeles Olympics as a member of the Canadian 4x100 relay team. When he returned home to Hamilton with his first Olympic medal, there was no welcoming committee or celebration. Two years later, he was part of the mile relay team that won a silver medal for Canada in the 1934 British Empire Games in London, England.

Ray Lewis spent 22 years on the road as a sleeping car porter. In spite of bringing international athletic recognition to Canada, it was the only job he could get. "I made the beds, and I shined the shoes. I cleaned the toilets, and I washed out the spittoons, which were very prominent in those days," he said. With no other facilities at his disposal, he trained by running alongside the train whenever it stopped. "Oft times in those days," he told *Hymn to Freedom* producer Speaks, "we would stop at different points for a single track to pass other trains coming down. And I would ask the train crew when we stopped how long would we be here. They'd tell me, 'Oh, we'll be here an hour waiting for number something-or-other coming in the opposite direction.' Then I would go in my car—the sleeper—put my track clothes on and do my jogging up and down beside the trains. I did this all across the country."

Ray Lewis died in November 2003, at the age of 93, having achieved, much later in life, recognition as an effective crusader for human rights. He was named to the Order of Canada in 2001. The citation states:

> He is the first Canadian-born Black athlete to
> stand at the victory podium and receive an Olympic
> medal in track and field. Training by running along-
> side the CP railway tracks and occasionally in farm-
> ers' fields, he was a member of the 4x400-metre relay
> team that won a bronze medal at the 1932 Olympic
> Games in Los Angeles and a silver medal at the 1934
> British Empire Games in London. He continues to
> be an inspiration to young people in the community,
> reminding them that dedication and commitment
> are values to be cherished.

Sleeping car porters earned steady, and for the times, respectable incomes. Many owned their own homes and insisted that their children get a good education. But the price for stable employment was finding a way to stomach the racism demonstrated both by passengers and by other railway workers. Displaying grit and determination, many sleeping car porters stayed with the job, some for 40 or more years. The skills and attitudes they developed to survive, both emotionally and sometimes physically, in a world in which they were often treated as subhuman, were transferred, by a kind of familial osmosis, to their children. In an era when "a man's home was his castle," their authority was unchallenged and, as both husbands and fathers, many became strict, by-the-book autocrats—a comprehensible reversal of the conditions they faced in their working lives.

An academic study of the impact that the challenges faced and met by sleeping car porters had on Canada's Black communities would provide valuable insights into the role played by their children and grandchildren. How could men whose working lives were so demeaning lead households and communities where the goal was to manifest the exact opposite of those harsh realities? They rarely brought their jobs home and worked hard to appear respectable to the world, both

Young Harry in football gear at North Vancouver High School. His speed helped him avoid being tackled.

inside and outside their households. The only places where they could talk freely about their working lives was in informal porters' clubs that sprang up and at the local barber shop, which became a Saturday afternoon gathering place, often sporting back rooms where patrons could socialize while their children were getting their hair cut.

The church played a powerful central role in railroad porter communities. Every Sunday, you put on your best clothes to attend services. Women and girls wore hats. Men and boys wore suits, carefully ironed white shirts and ties. Following church, Sunday afternoon picnics in summer, musical events and "socials" in winter, knit communities solidly together. Those who grew up in homes headed by porters were taught and admonished and taught again to do better. "You have to work twice as hard to prove your worth" was a common refrain pressed on children by both mothers and fathers. "You can use a degree like a club," Paul Winn's mother told him.

Your father might be putting up with God knows what on the railroad, and your mother might slip uptown several days a week to work as a maid in a rich household, but children were expected to get a good education, to do better. And, under no circumstances, were they ever to follow in their parent's footsteps. Jazz musician Joe Sealy says his father swore that none of his children would ever work on the railroad.

Harry Jerome Sr. endured discrimination throughout his working life. There is little doubt that the members of his household were aware of, and affected by, the racially biased environment that surrounded him and them. Their father was a fighter, not content to quietly accept the racism that confronted him. According to Elsie, he was suspended by the railroad at least three times, once for physically attacking a white passenger who had insulted him. Each time, he was able to talk his way back onto the road.

Like his father-in-law, Harry Jerome Sr. chose not to raise his family in one of the Black communities that surrounded major railroad centres. It was one way of seeking respectability, of providing a (hopefully) better environment in which your children could grow up and succeed. The Jeromes were living in Prince Albert, Saskatchewan, when Harry Jr. was born on September 30, 1940. He was still an infant when they moved to a house on Osborne Street in the East Kildonan area of Winnipeg and then, not long afterwards, bought a large house on Enfield Crescent in St. Boniface, a predominantly French-speaking enclave, where three more children, Carolyn, Barton and Valerie, were born. Harry attended a French-language school and took piano lessons. He went on occasional railroad trips with his father, rode his new bicycle, seemed to do well enough in school and generally appeared to be a happy but shy kid.

But Elsie didn't speak French, had few neighbourhood friends and received only occasional family visits. She felt lonely and isolated. With Harry Sr. away on the job much of the time, Elsie, still a young mother in her 20s, managed as best she could, planting a large garden and canning her produce. But she longed for a more congenial environment. Her marriage was becoming strained. She recalled being caught in the 1950 Red River flood, pregnant and alone with her children. They were evacuated from their home in the middle of the night, escaping in their pyjamas. It was, for her, a precipitating incident. She wanted to, needed to, move to a community where she could feel more at home and where her children would be comfortable.

In 1952, when Harry was 11, the family moved to North Vancouver. It was not Elsie's choice. She wanted to live in the more diverse community of East Vancouver, where they might find greater acceptance. But Harry Sr., according to his eldest daughter Carolyn, was determined to settle in North Vancouver, in a beautiful neighbourhood with good schools and manicured lawns. He wanted, like many trying to pull themselves out of a no-bed-of-roses background, a better environment and a better life for his children. At the end of the day, Elsie had no say in the matter but remained bitter about the choice for years. The move was designed to save a marriage facing rough water. And, for a few years, the family did hang together. But their lives would have been difficult under any circumstances. Elsie had married right off the farm and was 19 years younger than her husband.

Elsie's foreboding instincts about North Vancouver were soon borne out by a shattering reality.

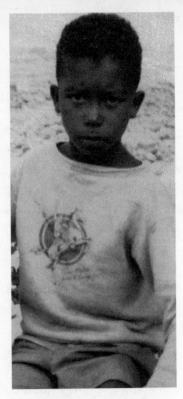

Chapter Three

Not Wanted
in the
Neighbourhood

…one hears the pain in their
voices as they begin to have second thoughts about
having moved out of the city into a mostly white suburb,
a move they made to protect their son from the possibility
of being caught in a gang shooting
and the certainty of attending an underfunded school.

–Barack Obama

As puberty looms, life is a quagmire of uncertainties, bewildering questions and quicksand challenges. Who am I? Where do I fit in this world? Do I really belong here? How can I understand the contradictions that I see all around me? Who can I trust, really trust? At 12, life can become almost overwhelmingly perplexing. We begin to see and question things we never thought about just a summer ago.

Harry Jerome was a sensitive, preteen adolescent when his family left St. Boniface for the West Coast. His father poured his savings into a heritage home located at 416 Lions Place in the City of North Vancouver. Young Harry could not help but know that his mother did not want to live there, that to live in a "nice" neighbourhood was his sleeping car porter father's dream. Before they could get properly settled, they were told that they should move. A woman who lived down the street had started a petition to force them out of the neighbourhood—a petition against, as Harry's sister Carolyn characterized it, "those coolies." The petition, raising all of the old myths about property values, incipient lawlessness and debauchery, got enough signatures from people in the neighbourhood to constitute a palpable threat. No one mentioned threats of violence, but behaviour inflamed by racial attitudes could be difficult to predict.

The Jeromes were not wanted in the neighbourhood.

Elsie was shattered. She went into a deep depression that Carolyn later described as a "funk that lasted a very long time." The rest of the family tried to cope. Harry Sr. demanded that the real estate company solve the problem. Young Harry, a 12-year-old trying hard to fit into a new school, was numbingly affected. Hurt and confused, he began the subconscious process of internalizing the racial demons that pursued him.

It's impossible to overemphasize the impact of this jolting rejection on a sensitive boy, still trying to understand where he fit in the

A high school class picture. Wendy said, "It was just a magnetism about him, an energy about him, a cleanness about him."

world. Today, it's a fairly well-known psychological phenomenon that people who suffer adversity, even though they are not in any way at fault, can nevertheless be overwhelmed by feelings that everything bad that happens is somehow their fault. One way of dealing with strong feelings of guilt and inadequacy is to build emotional walls to hide the way you feel from the outside world. The trouble with these barriers is that you're on the same side of the wall as the things that bedevil you. And, it seems, the higher you build the walls, the bigger and stronger the internal demons can become. So it should come as no surprise—not to indulge ourselves in pop-psychology analysis— that as he grew into adulthood, and especially when the sports world shone its most intense spotlight on him, Harry went to great lengths to keep his inner demons hidden and under control. One result was that he was often perceived by reporters as withdrawn, temperamental, non-communicative and, on occasion, explosively aggressive.

Patronizing attitudes are the most difficult to deal with. They are often subtle, displayed by people who may mean well, who really believe they that they are trying to be accommodating. They may pat you on the back but won't let you get too close. Paul Winn, in his foreword, is right when he says one of the litmus tests of how well you are really accepted comes when you show interest in their daughters. People who are patronizing usually fail to recognize what they're doing— but there is no doubt that those on the receiving end have finely tuned senses that pick up every unintended slur, every nuance of behaviour drawing a fine line between them and you. Too often, the incident has passed before the indignity sinks in, which creates even greater frustration—and middle-of-the-night rehearsals of what you should have said. Every minority individual (and every woman) knows this feeling. And yet, even late in his life, Harry Jerome protested to reporters that his colour was never a factor in his career. The facts, of course, do not match his assertions; they just illustrate the "stiff upper lip" he must have inherited from his grandmother. Carolyn remembers her brother as "a very quiet guy who did well in little league sports. He never caused trouble as a kid."

The realtor who had sold the house to the Jeromes, a firm called Irving and Billings, finally agreed to find a buyer for the house and to find a new home for them, hopefully in a more accommodating neighbourhood. But it still had to be, Harry Sr. insisted, in North Vancouver. The family finally moved to a house at 704 East 17th Avenue.

The neighbours turned out to be more tolerant, and that's where Harry spent his teen years. He was academically average. His grade nine Sutherland Junior High report card is dominated by Cs, with a smattering of Bs. His best subject was social studies. With an overall grade of C, denoting average, he was promoted to grade 10 at North Vancouver High School with the required number of credits. He graduated from North Van but failed his grade 12 English exam. In an early demonstration of his prickly resistance to anything he considered to be unjust, he responded by writing, in the student's comment section of the report card, that his English grades were "picky, unfair." But throughout his high school years, even as his prowess on the track emerged, his greater tendency was to keep his head down and avoid confrontation.

By the time he finished high school, Harry's athletic ability had already made him special. "Dear Mr. Jerome," said a December 30, 1959, letter from Harry M. Evans, head of the BC Office of the Registrar and Division of Examinations in Victoria. "Following conversation with your father yesterday, steps have been taken to give you the opportunity to fulfil university entrance requirements as expeditiously as possible. I have been in touch by telephone both yesterday and today with the Director of Admissions of the University of Oregon."

It seems that the senior Jerome had met BC Attorney General Robert Bonner, a passenger on his runs as a sleeping car porter, and had asked the minister to intervene. Harry, having broken Percy Williams' Olympic record earlier that year, had entered the ranks of elite athletes. Arrangements were made for Jerome to retake the English 40 course by correspondence. He was instructed to send the application forms directly to a Mr. Kershaw at the Correspondence Branch and to "mark the covering envelope 'Personal,' as Mr. Kershaw knows the circumstances and will expedite....I have suggested to your father," the letter went on, "that coaching continues to be available to you in the event you find need of it. This, of course, is a matter for decision by you and your father."

Wearing a North Van track tank top, Harry Jerome brings home the baton in the anchor leg of a relay race.

Two weeks later, a letter dated January 13, 1960, came from track coach Bill Bowerman, who had offered a scholarship at the University of Oregon, reporting that he had been contacted by the BC Department of Education about the decision to allow Harry to rewrite the exam: "From this, I gather that it is all set to issue you a notice of admission. When can I look forward to having you down?"

Harry passed the exam on April 1 and secured his admission to the University of Oregon.

In sharp contrast to the harsh treatment he received from the press through most of his career, this was the first of many incidents demonstrating that, in British Columbia in general and North Vancouver in particular, people stood behind Harry, offering him support through the ups and the downs of his career. But no Canadian university offered athletic scholarships. Canadians who excelled in sports could only find professional training and development support south of the border. When they participated in international sports in and on behalf of Canada, there was little support beyond a plane ticket and an allowance for meals and accommodation. Athletes' coaches were not encouraged, sometimes were not allowed, to travel with them. Team managers and other officials who accompanied Canada's athletes often had better political than sports credentials. American universities, on the other hand, poured huge resources into sports, offering increasingly lucrative scholarships and other perks to outstanding athletes who gave them national recognition and helped with their fundraising. So while Canada claimed Harry Jerome as its own, it was the Americans who gave him the training and support that allowed him to reach his full potential.

The "not wanted in the neighbourhood" petition was kept as a dark, and inappropriately shameful, family secret. One of Harry closest childhood friends, Ray Wickland, who lived nearby, was never told about it. Now a retired teacher living on BC's Galliano Island, Wickland remembers Jerome as shy and self-conscious. To him, the family was quite private, and he was never invited into their house. But through their junior high years, Ray and Harry walked to school together most days. Both boys had paper routes[11] and shared a self-defining commitment to sports. Young Harry, Ray remembered, loved to be physically active. Most of his friendships developed around sports. They played touch football, and though Wickland described him as still short, awkward and a bit gangly, he reported that Harry was a very good soccer player, later becoming a promising baseball pitcher, capable of throwing no-hitters and, with his developing speed, able to regularly beat the ball to first base after a bunt. On the gridiron, his speed overcame his aversion to being tackled.

"Harry was a late bloomer," Wickland said, "both socially and athletically. But he loved the outdoors and lost (and found) himself in sports." But Ray could also sense the family discord. He remembers Harry Sr. in his porter's uniform, nearly 20 years older than his wife, with curly, greying hair. Ray never heard him say a cross word, but he was distant. His memories of Elsie capture an image of a gregarious, friendly and supportive mother: "There was never a cloudy moment around her. She gave her kids the incentive to succeed."

Wickland grew to 183 centimetres tall and 91 kilograms and tried for a career in professional football. He was invited to the Winnipeg Blue Bombers training camp in 1963, the year after my brother Frank retired from the team. He was cut after the exhibition season and, being practical, went back to school to earn degrees in education. He went on to a career as a teacher.

The Jerome family faced tough internal challenges. Barton, the fourth child, was born during a traumatic time for the family, soon after the Winnipeg flood, just as they were getting ready for the move to Vancouver. It was a difficult birth, and doctors first said the child had just a 50/50 chance of surviving. Elsie was sent home and sent breast milk to the hospital on a regular schedule. The baby pulled through and developed into a physically healthy boy. But he had other problems.

By the time he entered elementary school, Barton was getting into a lot of trouble. He was marked with that damning label—"retarded." His parents tried to keep him at home, but when Elsie found herself pregnant with another daughter, Louise, the family doctor advised them to place Barton in Woodlands School, an institution that essentially warehoused the developmentally disabled, lowering both their expectations and those of their families. The Jeromes did not have a car, so they took Barton to the institution in an RCMP squad car. Little Carolyn, who watched them drive away with tears in her eyes, said, "It was a very sad day—and of course, they came home without him. There was no support, no one talked about it. We were just aware that Barton was gone. It was a horrible feeling, and one that to this day that causes me so much sadness that I get overwhelmed with it."

But Barton, intellectually limited, nevertheless had a big and forgiving heart, and as he grew up, he became quite enterprising. He couldn't read or write but was always able to find someone to write letters for him. Early in February 1960, he had a note written to "Mom and Dad" from the Woodlands School, thanking them for the wallet they gave him for Christmas and letting them know that he was fine. He was earning a little money shining shoes, he reported, and his only problem was that he wanted to smoke with the other boys, but the doctor wanted his parents' permission. Would they write to the doctor and let him know it was okay? And, by the way, the next time they came to visit, would they bring a colouring book and some crayons?

The family tried to keep Barton close, making the long trek out to Woodlands as often as they could manage. But Elsie had a new baby, and with her husband away on the road much of the time, the visits tapered off. Harry Sr. started spending more time in Vancouver after coming in from his railroad trips, hanging around the railroad porters' quarters on Keefer Street and developing a serious interest in horse racing. Elsie gardened, canned vegetables, made clothes for her children, got involved in church work and hung on.

Other members of the family had problems, too. Carolyn suffered from epileptic seizures. In March 1960, she went out into their backyard wearing only light clothing, and a powerful convulsion struck without warning, throwing her to the ground. She fell so hard, she dislocated her shoulder. She was unconscious for two hours in near-freezing weather; no one in the house noticed that she was gone. When she regained consciousness, she thumped on the door, and Elsie rushed her to the hospital. Carolyn left home as a teenager, became

Harry Jerome Sr. with his family's two star athletes, Harry Jr. and Valerie.

the mother of two girls and learned how to survive. Today, her seizures under control, she and her partner live comfortably on Galliano
Island and operate an attractive bed-and-breakfast facility.

Louise, shy and quiet, the baby of the family, works as a caregiver
in Vancouver.

Valerie, a promising athlete in her youth, became an Olympian and represented Canada at several international track events.

North Vancouver in the 1950s and 1960s, was a white-collar bedroom community. Harry was probably the only Black kid at Sutherland Junior High. At North Vancouver High School, which then had a student population of about 900, you could count on your fingers the number of non-white students. Paul Angelo Winn was Harry Jerome's early running mate and best friend. By his count, there were two Japanese boys, one Japanese girl, an East Indian boy, one Black girl and Harry and Paul.

No one knew Harry better than Paul Winn, who Wickland described as "the lawyer" of the North Vancouver High School student community. Winn did, in fact, became a lawyer later in life, going back to university in his 50s to earn his degree and admittance to the British Columbia bar. Winn is a smiling, bearded bear of a man. But this bear has claws and has become a nationally recognized anti-discrimination fighter. He is a director and former chair of the board of the Canadian Race Relations Foundation and a successful Vancouver businessman. Never as committed an athlete as Jerome, he nevertheless had enough natural talent to succeed in high school athletics and beyond. "I had kangaroo legs, which made me a good jumper," he joked. "Just as well, because Harry and I didn't have to compete head to head with each other."

Paul was 16 the summer he moved from Toronto to Vancouver. His father, who had also been a sleeping car porter, died when he was five, leaving his mother to raise a family in which he was the sixth of 10 children. In 1956, his mother found an opportunity for him to go to school in Vancouver under the watchful eye of social worker John Braithwaite. Concerned that her feisty kid was going to get into serious trouble in their inner-city neighbourhood, near what is now Kensington market, Winn's mother persuaded Braithwaite to become her son's official guardian until he reached the age of majority, which in those days was 21.

Braithwaite had himself been a star athlete, a member of a Toronto team that won the 1952 Canadian men's basketball title. He was moving to Vancouver to become executive director of Vancouver's North Shore Neighbourhood House, a position he held for 23 years.[12] He spent 17 years as a member of Vancouver's city council and was a suitable role model for the young, adventurous Winn. Paul remembered the drive across the country with his guardian as a great adventure. They had the opportunity for long, serious talks, and Winn absorbed some of Braithwaite's strong sense of social responsibility. When they got to Vancouver, Braithwaite found him a place to live with Winnie and Stan Henderson, who lived not far from the Jeromes in North Vancouver. The couple were ardent supporters of the socialist CCF party and had no problem taking in a Black kid from Toronto, reported to be a bit of a handful. They took him to political meetings, giving him an early introduction to political activism. He absorbed values that have animated his attitudes through much of his career in athletics and beyond.

As much as Harry Jerome was shy and unsure of himself, Paul Winn was a confident, assertive teenager who never backed down from anything or anyone. By the time he arrived in Vancouver, he was already a star athlete in his own right, holding a number of Canadian student records in the triple jump. He quickly became a popular member of the student body and was soon elected to student council while continuing to win medals in track and field.

He was what you would describe today as a kid who was always "in your face." When the principal of their North Vancouver school saw him standing in a group of students with his arm around a white girl, he banged furiously on the window and ordered Winn into his office. "Whenever you talk to any female in this school," he roared, echoing ancient primal fears about racial purity, "I want you to stand three feet away." Young Winn was not intimidated. The next day, he brought a yardstick to school and "anytime I was talking to any female, including teachers, I'd put the stick out," he recalled. "I'm just following

Harry at North Vancouver High School. He started running very fast when he was 17, capturing scores of medals and trophies through a long career on the track.

(W.R.) McDougall's instructions," he would explain. He kept it up for several days, and McDougall never mentioned the incident again.

It took a while for Harry and Paul to warm up to each other. "We kind of circled each other," Paul recalled. "Harry found it a bit uncomfortable to be around me at first. He dressed conservatively...used to comb his hair like a white kid. I was wearing hip Toronto clothes, suede shoes and pants with buckles on the back. And I could dance." Harry, unable to let himself go, to yield to the abandon that is essential to real dancing, could not. While Jerome tended to keep a low profile and avoid controversy or confrontation, Winn rose with relish to every challenge. He was about to get into a fight with a boy who was, until Winn came on the scene, the school's athletic idol: "I wasn't all that fast, but I was way faster than him." The boy, jealous and a bully, had gathered a group of his friends, and they had Winn cornered. The fight was about to begin when a couple of hefty senior student football players intervened. Winn remarked to me that it was a racial issue. The seniors put the bully on notice. "We're not like that here," they said.

Winn was a year older than Jerome but had "flunked" a grade along the way, so they were in the same class. They were together in a social studies class whose teacher also coached the rugby team and, realizing how fast they were, put them on his team. They got to know each other by sharing the team spirit, going on to play on baseball and football teams and ultimately starring in track and field.

The pair ran together on 4x100-yard relay teams. Paul would run the first leg, and Harry would bring it home as anchor, often with high school buddies Jim McKay and Don Basham in between. About racing one on one against each other, Winn said, "On any given day any one of us could win. More often than not it was Harry, but there was no great gap." In fact, Winn was faster off the blocks than Jerome and would often be ahead for the first 25 yards. But by the time they reached the halfway mark, Harry was usually ahead.

Paul and Harry were now spending a lot of their time together, training and sharing a robust team spirit. The two fastest kids in North Vancouver High, Winn made sure I noted, were Black. There were odd, sometimes laughable, consequences. On one occasion, Harry and Paul teamed up with a pair of twin brothers, Dave and Jim McKay. Paul, as usual, started off, and Harry ran the anchor with the white twins running the second and third legs of the 4x100. After they won, someone protested, apparently quite seriously, that they had only put two men in the race—a Black guy and a white guy. The Black guy, they charged, after running the first leg, ran across the infield to anchor the race, while the white guy ran the two middle legs. The idea was ludicrous, of course, and the complaint was dismissed.

And they were popular. Paul led the way, organizing lunchtime sock hops, acting as disc jockey, playing (45 rpm) records and teaching students how to jive. His 1958 high school yearbook, in which he appears as a member of student council, is signed by more girls than boys. He was once invited to a Sadie Hawkins[13] dance by Heather Sinclair, the older sister of Margaret Trudeau, and was later invited to their home. Their father was then the federal minister of fisheries. "I was living a life like a young, white, suburban kid," Paul reminisced. "Harry was living this, too, but I was more aggressive."

Exotic in the North Vancouver school community, Paul set trends in fashion and behaviour and dated white girls. He had worn a moustache since before his arrival in Vancouver, and when other male students began to follow his example, Principal McDougall again summoned him to his office. "If many other boys start growing moustaches, you'll have to shave yours off," the principal declared. Not intimidated, Paul pointed out that he'd already been in the school for more than a year. "Why was he bringing this up now?" Again, McDougall dropped the issue.

Harry would sometimes date girls that Paul had taken out. Years later, Winn reported, someone told him that Harry figured that if the girls went out with Paul, they'd go out with him. "He was shy, there was a lot of racism in the school, and they were a safe bet."

Winn was a regular visitor to the Jerome household, almost a member of the family, which, at that point, was reasonably cohesive. "I missed being around a Black family." A third daughter, Louise, had come along, but it was by now clear that Harry's younger brother, Barton, was, in today's parlance, intellectually challenged. Harry seemed embarrassed about his "retarded" brother, the stigma hanging heavily

Harry Jerome and BC team with trophy

over the family. Barton was still at home, undiagnosed and always getting into trouble in school. But Paul liked and accepted him, and they got along well. "One year I gave him a wallet for his birthday," he reminisced. "It was probably more cardboard than leather, but Barton thought it was the 'cat's meow.' He was a big, strong kid, and he liked to punch you in a way that he thought was playful. He was probably about seven or eight mentally, so he'd punch you like an eight-year-old, but he had the strength of a man."

Barton was eventually moved to an institution called Tranquille, a home for the mentally handicapped near Kamloops, BC. There, it was later learned, he, like other males, was castrated; females were sterilized. Years later, a woman known publicly only by the initials of L.S. successfully sued the BC government, alleging she was sterilized at the age of 15 without consent. The home closed in 1984, and the residents were dispersed into group homes and the wider community. It wasn't until 2003 that the government of British Columbia issued a formal apology for the heartless treatment to which inmates had been subjected.

Barton, whatever his circumstances, was part of the stand-up-for-yourself Jerome gene pool. He fought his institutionalization with surprising might, persuading friends to mount a letter campaign to the premier to complain that he was being badly treated. The campaign was eventually successful, and Barton was able to leave the institution and to live successfully on his own. He walked into a Kelowna Plymouth-Chrysler dealership one day and offered to shovel snow. There was no snow on the ground, but Barton was planning ahead. Steady and reliable, he ended up sweeping and shovelling there for nearly 10 years. Co-workers referred to him as "Mr. Vice President." "Work all day, work all night," he liked to say.

Car man Ernie Falk was boss to the tall, gangling man-boy with the wide, winning grin. "The handicapped, the disenfranchised, also have a place in society," Falk said. "Barton Jerome wanted to be self-supporting, and he wanted to be part of the community. He said a couple of times, 'I'm out in the community, and I'm doing good, aren't I?' He always chased down extra work, mowing lawns, washing windows, collecting bottles."

Barton was careful with his money and saved enough to buy his own mobile home. With friends doing the paperwork, he paid taxes, had a girlfriend and enjoyed doing jigsaw puzzles. He knew, according to Paul Winn, exactly the level of difficulty that he could manage and never bought puzzles that were beyond his ability. And he loved church. The afternoon before he died, he helped deliver Bibles as part of a "Bibles for All" program.

When Barton came to Vancouver, he often stayed with Paul Winn. But it was while he was still in the institution that he became the source of one of the few big disagreements between Paul and Harry.

In addition to seven world records, Harry Jerome won scores of other trophies, medals and ribbons.

They were attending a track meet in Kelowna not far from the Tranquille institution, and Paul wanted to visit Barton. Harry, embarrassed by his younger brother, refused to go. Paul went alone.

It created a chill between them that lasted for some time.

Winn said that Barton loved Harry and kept lots of pictures of his big brother on the walls of his trailer home. Harry did not treat him badly, he said, often sending him gifts. "But it was a distant caring."

Barton was riding his bicycle on a highway on April 23, 1989, when he was hit by a truck and killed.[14]

Chapter Four

How Fast is Fast?

*I was trying to raise myself
to be a black man
in America, and beyond the given
of my appearance,
no one around me seemed to know
exactly what that meant.*

–Barack Obama

In the beginning, the sprint *was* the Olympics. It was the only event in the first 13 times the event was held, then as now, every four years. Runners sprinted the length of the stadium (from the word "stadion"; a "stade" was 192 metres) and back. A wooden post, apparently to help runners make a quick turn, was set up at one end of the stadium. Men started from a standing position with their toes lined up on grooves in a stone starting line, and ran naked, their bodies glistening with olive oil. If a runner made a false start, he was likely to be flogged on the spot by a judge standing behind the starting line. It was important to "toe the line," and that well-worn phrase may well have had its origins in the early Olympics.

The first recorded Olympic victor, traditionally dated to 776 BC, was Koroibos, a cook from a town named Elis. He received no monetary reward, just a crown of olive leaves. But then, and now, the fastest man achieved instant celebrity. Winners were given front-row seats at important events, could eat free in the great establishments of the day and had the right to have a statue of themselves erected at Olympia.

The Greeks believed that harmonious movement was important, so athletes often exercised to music. They trained hard; their trainers used staffs to point out incorrect body positions. They paid close attention to balancing physical exercise with diet.

When Baron Pierre de Coupertin persuaded Georgios Averoff to put up one million Greek drachmas to fund the first modern games in Athens in 1896, 285 athletes from 13 countries competed. The centrepiece of the event was the 100-metre sprint. The race was won by an American, Francis Lane, of Princeton, in 12.2 seconds. The 100-metre race has remained at the top of the podium of elite sports ever since. Whoever holds the record is acknowledged as the "fastest human in the world."

John Minichiello and Milton Wong were not much older than Harry Jerome and Paul Winn when, in 1957, they decided to form a track club. Wong demonstrated an early entrepreneurial ability by persuading the Optimists Service Club to fund the initiative. Milton was the manager; John was the coach. Minichiello had discovered Harry, Paul and a small group of other North Vancouver athletes, including Ray Wickland, at a relay race. "Harry wasn't the anchor, Paul was," he reminisced. "But it was Harry who'd given them a great start." They recruited Jerome, Winn and Harry's sister Valerie (Harry asked, "Can I bring my sister?"[15]) along with Wickland and others to join the club. Jerome was the club's star athlete—their best performer in the 100 yards, 100 metres, 220 yards and 200 metres. Paul Winn led in the hop, skip and jump. Valerie led in the 100 yards, 100 metres, 60 metres, broad jump and high jump.

The Optimist Striders went on to become one of the most successful BC track teams of its era. Milton Wong went on to become a highly successful money manager with the Hong Kong Bank and its successor, HSBC. When I met him in his office in the HSBC Tower in the heart of downtown Vancouver, I expected to find a busy, high-pressure businessman in a three-piece suit, with little time to spare for authors writing about events long since passed. Instead, I found a casually dressed, warm, open and committed community activist whose current preoccupation—business aside—was helping to improve the lives of people in Vancouver's down-on-its-luck East Side. He told me stories of trips to track meets they had taken in his station wagon; Harry was always a kind of backseat driver, telling Milton which turns to take and urging him to "pass that guy." Once, Wong recalled, on the way to a track meet in Saskatoon, he took Harry's advice on a crowded highway and barely got back into his lane to avoid oncoming traffic. "It was pretty scary," and Harry didn't urge him to pass anyone for the rest of the trip. We spent a pleasant hour talking about the importance of Harry Jerome's contributions to Canada, and it was I, not he, who ended the interview.

Both Milton Wong and John Minichiello became important citizens in the BC Lower Mainland. They were among the founders of the

Laurier Institution, a Vancouver think tank created in 1989 by business and community leaders to advance and disseminate knowledge about the economic and social implications of Canadian diversity. Both are still listed as directors. In 1994, Wong was recognized as Vancouver's Socially Responsible Entrepreneur of the Year.

Minichiello, alongside a 35-year career in education and community service, including service as a member of the City of Vancouver Planning Commission, was a world-class track coach. He was selected coach of the Canadian International Team sent to Cuba in 1964, the Pan American Games Team of 1967, the European Tour Team of 1968 and the Olympic Team of 1968. He served as a director of the BC Track and Field Coaches Award Plan and the Canadian Track and Field Association and was later chair of the Harry Jerome Commemorative Society. I met him at his home in Richmond. A diminutive man with a steady gaze and a strong, well-modulated voice, he projected both warmth and authority. He was coach, mentor and friend to Harry Jerome throughout his running career and beyond. It was he who encouraged Harry to do serious weight training at a time when other coaches, including the University of Oregon's storied track coach, Bill Bowerman, thought that weight training was not an appropriate regime for runners.

It wasn't until after his 17th birthday that Jerome experienced a spurt in his growth and began to develop the fluid, graceful movement that would trademark his running.

Almost overnight, as his body matured, Harry Jerome started approaching world-record times. In 1958, the Optimist Striders competed in a North American universities track meet at Vancouver's Empire Stadium. They were the only non-university team competing—all their members were still in high school. In the continent-wide competition, they came second to the University of Nebraska, setting a new world high school record in the 4x100.

Harry Jerome's record, in the eight years that followed—an exceptionally long run in the life of a sprinter—established him as one of

This photo was taken in the run-up to the 1962 British Empire and Commonwealth Games in Perth, Australia. "He was a beautiful runner to watch. He was so gifted, such a fine competitor, and he ran so smoothly," said Bruce Kidd.

the best track athletes that Canada has ever produced. As the athletic world became aware of Harry, it opened up for him. The Optimists Striders Track Team was probably the best track team in Canada, its members regularly breaking records. University scholarships beckoned. It was, in many ways, a golden time in his life. But it hadn't started out that way.

"It was funny," he told *Toronto Star* reporter Jim Hunt early in his career, "but I quit running as a juvenile because I couldn't beat anyone. I was too small to play football and couldn't hit well enough in baseball, so running seemed like the only sport. But as a juvenile, I was a flop—couldn't even place in a high school meet."

Throughout his life, Harry kept a strict division between his life on the track and his life with his friends. On the track, he was all business, driven by the seriousness he brought to his training. Track always came first—no question. When he and Paul Winn lived together during the 1960s, he would often come home at night after a movie and ask Paul if he had trained that day. If Winn answered in the negative, Harry, taking charge, would say, "Come on, let's go." And they would be out in the dark, sometimes in the rain, running Brockton Oval in Stanley Park, running up Grouse Mountain, sometimes backwards, running in the sand at Spanish Banks Beach or practising starts at some lonely track.

Sport was his life, and his circle of sporting friends was as much his family as his parents and siblings; in fact, given the evidence, more so. But university life in Oregon was a mixed blessing. The University of Oregon was one of several American universities that sought Harry out when he started breaking records. Oregon, with the legendary Bill Bowerman as coach, had one of the best college track teams in the U.S. Bowerman offered scholarships to both Harry and Paul Winn, but the proposition for Winn, competing as a jumper, was for only a partial scholarship. Paul didn't have the resources to support himself in Oregon on partial funding and opted to continue his studies at the University of British Columbia. Bowerman, as it happened, was not the only one in Oregon who wanted Harry. In an August 19, 1959, letter, Sam Bell, track coach at the Department of Intercollegiate Athletics at Oregon State University at Corvallis, Oregon, wrote:

> I understand that you are to talk to Mr. Bower-
> man back at the Pan Am games, and when you do
> talk with him, I want you to consider just what he is
> offering you in the line of scholarships. I know that
> it will involve at least 40 hours of work a month,
> and, in your case, I feel that you would be a lot bet-
> ter off in a program where you would not have to
> work so much. I know that they will also tell you
> that it doesn't take much time, and that it is just as if
> you would not have to do it, but you will find that
> this is not the case, I believe. ....I would certainly like
> to have you in our program, Harry, and I am sure
> that if you have passed your English exam, we will
> be able to work something out.

Jerome declined the offer and spent the rest of his student life in the university town of Eugene, earning both an undergraduate and a master's degree in physical education at the University of Oregon. He quickly became the star of the Oregon University Ducks, frequently referred to in the local media as the "webfoot tracksters." Harry, perhaps as a silent declaration of independence, began to wear his Oregon track shirts inside out, so that OREGON appeared as NOGERO, which many took as a glancing reference to "Negro." But he never explained his reasons. "There's no reason for it," he would say. "It's just to make people ask questions. Just for the heck of it, really."

Bill Bowerman had a reputation as a great technical coach, creating the hard-day/easy-day training regime. His teams won four National Collegiate Athletic Association (NCAA) championships; his athletes set 13 world records and 22 American records. Twenty-three of his students went to the Olympics. He capped his career as coach of the

Harry preparing for a track meet at the University of Oregon.

U.S. team for the 1972 Munich Olympics. But Harry Jerome's home-town coach, John Minichiello, stayed involved, encouraging him in his weight training, something the Oregon coach didn't believe in at the time. Bowerman changed his mind when he saw the results, and it is fitting that the weight room at the University of Oregon is now named for Harry Jerome.

To create an advantage for his runners, Bowerman began to create handmade track shoes. Very lightweight, they were like slippers with spikes and rarely lasted for more than one race, but they were the start of something big. One story, which may be apocryphal, says that Bowerman was having a breakfast of waffles with his wife in a restaurant when he got what turned out to be a brilliant idea. He went home and started pouring latex rubber into his wife's waffle iron. The increasingly successful result was the development of strong but lightweight soles for his shoes, which, as it turned out, also provided better traction. In 1962, he and Phil Knight, a former middle-distance runner on Bowerman's University of Oregon track team, each put up $500 to create a partnership that eventually became Nike. Harry Jerome, among others, was invited to invest, but Harry, on the advice of a friend, businessman Konrad Tittler, declined. "If Harry had lived, he would probably have killed me by now," Tittler said years later. "That investment would have made him a multi-millionaire."

Bowerman and his partners started selling shoes out of the back of a van at school track meets in 1965. And the rest, as they say...Today, Nike is the largest sports apparel company in the world. The Massachusetts Institute of Technology has recognized Bill Bowerman as the inventor of the modern athletic shoe.

Bowerman died in his sleep on Christmas Eve 1999. He was 88.

While Jerome always competed for Canada in international races, it was as a member of Bowerman's Ducks that he gained experience and matured as an athlete. Bowerman was a hard and tricky taskmaster and used every ploy in the book to help his charges to victory. He told Jerome to "hate" his racing opponents, to totally obliterate them on the track. "I hate everybody I'm running against," Harry confided to Paul Winn. He often used surprising tactics, given his shyness, to unnerve his competition. At the Jamaica Commonwealth Games, Konrad Tittler, there to cheer him on, tells a story that may have been typical of the methods Jerome would use to "psyche out" his opponents. The day before the 100-metre final race, when a sprinter named Lennox Miller was practising his starts, Harry would, as casually as possible and seemingly pretending that he didn't even know his opponent was there, come up and set his starting blocks a metre or so behind him. Lennox would get set in his blocks, and just as he was about to burst out, Harry would fly by him. "He did this several times," Tittler said, "and the guy, who was younger, never protested."

While Harry "hated" his opponents during races, off the track, many of his fellow athletes became friends. But, even off track, Jerome was nothing, if not competitive. Journalist Brian Pound tells the story of being in a room one Saturday night during an intense card game between three of the fastest runners in the world—Harry Jerome, Bob Hayes and Jamaican Erwin Roberts—all in Oregon for the NCAA championships. The competition between them was so passionate, he said, "that I thought it would have ended up in a fist fight. I thought that I was sitting on the biggest sports story of my life—'NCAA sprint cancelled because runners in fist fight.' But they cooled down and, of course, I couldn't write the story."

Jerome's competitiveness was also illustrated when he would come to Pound's home, bringing some board game he liked to play. Pound's wife would consistently beat him at it—whereupon Harry would get up, take his game and stomp out of the house.

A brief overview of Jerome's major competitive accomplishments, and his two great mishaps, will set the stage for the rest of the story (a complete record of Jerome's track accomplishments is included in Appendix III, page 227):

- March 13, 1959: North Vancouver High School, North Vancouver, BC
  Jerome equals Percy Williams' Inter High School record for the 100-yard dash in a time of 10 seconds flat.

- May 27, 1959: Empire Stadium, Vancouver, BC
  Eighteen-year-old Jerome breaks Percy Williams' 31-year-old world record for the 200 metres, established at 22 seconds flat in the 1928 Olympics. Jerome covers the distance in 21.9 seconds. Williams, who would become Jerome's friend and hero, also won the 100-metre sprint in the same Olympics, clocking

Harry and Percy Williams in a 1959 photo, arranged by journalist Brian Pound, shortly after he broke Percy's record for the 220-yard dash, a record Williams had established in 1928.

10.8 seconds. He was the first Canadian athlete to win double gold at the Olympics. (The second was Donovan Bailey, who made his mark at the 1996 Atlanta Olympics.) It was shortly after this event that Harry's coach, John Minichiello, took him to Eugene, Oregon, to compete in a meet against some of the better American sprinters. He won the 100-yard dash in 9.5 seconds, setting a new record.

- July 16, 1960: Canadian Olympic Trials, Griffith Stadium Track, Saskatoon, Saskatchewan
  Jerome runs the 100 metres in 10.0 seconds, tying a world record set earlier that year by an unusual German runner,

Harry breaks the tape running for Bill Bowerman's University of Oregon track team.

Armin Hary.[16] Their record stood for eight years, until Jim Hines ran the distance in 9.9 seconds in the 1968 semifinals of the American Athletic Union (AAU) championships in Sacramento, California.

In July, 1963, the Saskatchewan Branch of the Amateur Athletic Union of Canada set a plaque in Griffiths Stadium, commemorating Jerome's achievement. "You've helped to put Saskatoon on the map," wrote Track and Field Chairman Bob Adams. One observer noted wryly that when officials measured the track, they found it to be one-quarter inch higher at the end than at the beginning. Jerome was running uphill, he said, something he did, figuratively, all of his life.

- May 20, 1961: Bell Field, Corvallis, Oregon
Jerome runs the 100 yards in 9.3 seconds, equalling the world record set by Mel Patton in 1948. He became the first man to

co-hold world records for both the 100-yard and 100-metre sprints.

- August 25, 1962: Empire Stadium, Vancouver, BC
Jerome runs 100 yards in 9.2 seconds, equalling a new world record set by both Bob Hayes and Frank Budd earlier that year.

- October 15, 1964: Olympic Games, Tokyo, Japan
Jerome wins the bronze medal in the 100-metre race with a time of 10.2. The feat is generally acknowledged as one of the greatest comebacks in track and field history. He ran fourth in the 200 metres, clocking 20.8 seconds, finishing just out of the medals.

- July 15, 1966: Canadian Track and Field Championships, Edmonton, Alberta
Len Corben, a sports columnist as well as Coordinator of Athletics for North Shore Secondary Schools until he retired in 1999, covered the event for the Vancouver papers. He wrote:

ID card for the 1964 Olympics in Tokyo, Japan. Harry won the bronze medal in the 100-metre race, staging one of the greatest comebacks in track and field history.

These are moments to remember. Thrills that last a lifetime. Friday evening at the University of Alberta track was one of those moments. ...Almost 300 athletes were contesting the Canadian championships and the right to go to the British Empire Games in Kingston, Jamaica. ...Now the runners were down...then set...and away. Jerome was in front on the first stride. ...Thirty yards out, he was all alone. At 50 yards, it was obvious he wasn't going to coast home on this one. His face, which usually expresses unconcern, now reflected determination. Sensing this, the crowd rose as one with a shout of excitement and encouragement. Jerome hit the finish line like a human knife, splitting the wool tape in two with such force it sprung back to the finish poles lake an elastic band. You knew it was going to be extra special.

The official timers huddled for 10 minutes before announcing the result as 9.1 seconds, matching the record set by Jerome's great rival, Bob Hayes of the U.S. That record would stand until 1974, long after Jerome had retired from competition.

- August 1966: British Empire and Commonwealth Games, Kingston, Jamaica

  Harry Jerome wins the gold medal an injury had not allowed him to capture in the 1962 games. He matches his Canadian time, running the 100-yard dash in 9.1 seconds. With Armin Hary permanently out of running because of a leg injury and Hayes having left sprinting for football, Harry Jerome, holding the world records for both the 100-metre and the 100-yard sprints, was the fastest man in the world. The next day he ran 220 yards in 20.4, one-tenth of a second off the new world record of 20.3.

IDENTITY CARD
Tarjeta de Identidad
Winnipeg, Manitoba
Canada 1967
V PAN AMERICAN GAMES
JUEGOS DEPORTIVOS PANAMERICANOS

Family Name ___JEROME___
Apellidos (Please print—Letras mayúsculas)

Given Name ___HARRY___
Nombre (Please print—Letras mayúsculas)

Category ___ATHLETICS___
Posicion

Organizing Committee for the **V Pan American Games**
Comite Organizador de los **V Juegos Panamericanos**

2756

Executive Director
Director Ejecutivo

ID card issued for the 1967 Pan American Games. Harry won gold in the 100-metre sprint not long before his 27th birthday. By this age, most sprinters have retired.

- July 31, 1967: Pan American Games, Winnipeg, Manitoba
  On a warm, drizzly day, Jerome wins the gold medal for the 100 metres with a time of 10.2 seconds.

- October 1968: Olympic Games, Mexico City, Mexico
  Jerome, aged 28, old for a sprinter, and four others, finish the 100 metres with an official time of 10.1 seconds. Jerome is awarded seventh place. Sports experts say that, even with the differences afforded by Mexico City's 2250-metre-high altitude, a more modern track and the latest hi-tech footwear, it was remarkable for Jerome to come within one-tenth of a second of the world record he had achieved eight years earlier.

That's a thumbnail sketch at Jerome's major wins. He won scores of medals at local, regional and international track meets around the world, posting more world records than any other sprinter of his era.

But there were two races that Harry Jerome did not win:

- August 1960: Olympic Games, Rome, Italy
  The favourites for the 100-metre sprint were the joint world record holders, Armin Hary and Harry Jerome. In the first semifinal, Jerome was in the lead, when he pulled a muscle and was unable to finish. Hary won the second semifinal and prepared for the September 1 final. After three false starts, in which he twice beat the gun, Hary won the race in 10.2 seconds.

Canadian sportswriters had gone to great lengths hyping the race, creating the certain expectation that Jerome would bring home the gold medal. He was, at 19, their new champion, the up-and-coming Canadian hero. But when he pulled a muscle and had to retire, Canadian newspaper headlines were anything but kind. Sportswriters accused him of being a quitter, not capable of competing in the "big" races. Jerome was combative in his responses to the media but, as much as possible, kept his own counsel. The sports establishment began to describe him as difficult, haughty, a bad interview.

Harry crossing the finish line—first, as usual—at Hayward Field at the University of Oregon in Eugene.

- November 24, 1962: British Empire and Commonwealth Games, Perth, Australia

  It was at the British Empire Games in Perth that the controversy surrounding Jerome reached its most ruinous low. The 1962 Games were noted for extreme temperatures, which reached 40°C during the opening ceremonies. It was 39°C the day Jerome experienced the major disaster of his running career. As he raced for gold, halfway through the race, a virtually shredded pair of muscles in his left leg made him go "all wobbly," and he finished last. He had severed the quadriceps muscles in his left leg. The question was not whether he might race again, but whether he would be able to walk normally.

  "Jerome Folds Again" ran the headline above Allan Fotheringham's front-page story in the *Vancouver Sun*. Jerome was devastated by the negative treatment frequently piled on him, almost gang-style, by the sports establishment. There was nothing in his experience that could have prepared him for the overwhelming impact of the media coverage that dogged his life and career.

But there was another, more poignant side to his life.

Chapter Five

A Husband and a Father

*Miscegenation. The word is humpbacked,
ugly, portending a monstrous outcome:
like antebellum or octoroon, it evokes images of
another era, a distant world of horsewhips and flames,
dead magnolias and crumbling porticos.*

–Barack Obama

They met at the University of Oregon in the fall of 1960. He, the international track star; she, a smart, pretty redhead from Edmonton studying sports psychology. Their relationship was star-crossed from the beginning, buffeted by the palpable hostility of the 1960s towards interracial relationships. Laws forbidding miscegenation were still on the books in Oregon. The debate then was as virulent and as polarized as today's turbulent confrontations over same-sex marriage.

Wendy Carole Foster, 22, smart and attractive, born and raised in Edmonton, had completed her undergraduate degree in physical education at the University of Alberta and had taught for a year at the city's Ross Sheppard High School. She was a competitive badminton player and coach—an athlete in her own right. Deciding to pursue a master's degree, she applied and was admitted to the University of Oregon at Eugene on the recommendation of the legendary Dr. Maury Van Vliet, dean of the Faculty of Physical Education and Recreation at the University of Alberta.

Harry Jerome had returned from the Rome Olympics to continue work on his undergraduate degree and to run for Bill Bowerman's team, then among the top track teams in the U.S. He was still smouldering from the treatment he had received from the press over not winning in Rome and was determined to do better at the British Empire Games, coming up in 1962.

Harry, on a full scholarship, was living in the athletic dormitory. Wendy was rooming with a family downtown and had part-time work as a teaching assistant. With fairly typical Canadian prairie idealism, in which racial prejudice was not a factor, Wendy was of course aware of, and curious about, Harry Jerome. She wanted to meet him. She asked a friend to arrange an introduction, and they met in the university library on September 30, his 20th birthday.

Harry and Wendy during happy days at their home in Eugene, Oregon.

Sparks flew. "He was very attractive physically," she said, decades after the fact. "If you took him apart piece by piece, he wasn't that handsome, but it was just a magnetism about him, an energy about him, a cleanness about him." She was well aware of, and had strong feelings about, the way the press had covered him at the Olympics. "I felt Rome was wrong. I have a defiant streak. I'd die for a principle." They found themselves agreeing about things athletic, and about their shared anger towards the sports press.

They started dating right away. Nothing extraordinary. They were young, and it was 1960, a time when many their age still thought they could solve all of the world's problems—really believed they could turn the planet into a garden. John Kennedy, still a U.S. senator, had launched the Peace Corps, which encouraged young Americans to go out and save the world. Saving the world, at least for Wendy, included meeting the challenges of racism. Harry was more closed on the subject. He had demons of shame and guilt to hide.

In an environment where others did more than frown at them, they were defiantly open about their relationship. They would go hand in hand to buy ice cream cones, to the movies and to sports events. A lot of the time they just walked and talked through Eugene's leafy parks and neighbourhoods, where you can imagine the wives of good burghers peering from behind curtains and clucking their disapproval. In liberal, far-from-the-Deep-South Oregon, the harassment started right away. Fellow athletes on the track team told Harry they shouldn't go out together in public. It was okay, they would tell him, to "fool around" with white girls, to treat them the way stars always treated what we now describe as "groupies," but you were not allowed to have a serious, certainly not a public, relationship. But Wendy was no groupie trying to find her own identity in someone famous. She was a "somebody" who was already developing her own distinguished career. But she recognized his talent, was attracted to it and wanted to share in it.

In the face of it, the two young idealists met the adversities with defiance. It was almost inevitable that these proud, competitive and stubborn kids would fall in love. "The word 'love' hadn't passed between us yet, but I really liked him," Wendy recalled. "I found him in many ways emotionally needy. And you know women like to be around men who are emotionally needy. He had lots of friends, but I don't think Harry let a lot of people in very close. I don't think he knew how to get close to people. He had a wall and, even with me, he'd let it down sometimes, but then the wall would go up again...almost as if he was afraid to be hurt." Harry, on the other hand, at the time described Wendy to some of his friends, perhaps as much in self-defence as anything else, as "kinda clingy." She was the active partner in the relationship. Harry, with his locked up emotions, was more passive, not quite sure how to handle the intensity of this—according to his closest friends—his first real relationship with a woman.

Coach Bowerman made it clear that he disapproved and was allegedly a party to, if not the author of, an intervention that tried to force the couple apart. According to Wendy, the university's Athletic Department put pressure on the Education Department to revoke her teaching assistant job because she was "an inappropriate role model."

"All kinds of things started to happen," she said. "My car would be towed out of the parking lot. If I left the windows open, it would be filled with garbage. They told me flat out that if I didn't stop seeing Harry, I wouldn't be able to teach any more. I was put in the office, filing."

When she got home one evening, Wendy collapsed in a storm of exasperated tears. The open-minded couple whose home she boarded at were appalled when they heard her story. They had some influence in the community and called the university chancellor to let him know what was going on. He intervened, telling the Athletic Department to "cut it out." The harassment, at least in its most overt forms, stopped, but the disapproval remained palpable, if more subtle.

Their best times, Wendy remembered, were their early days of dating in Oregon. But they were both extremely competitive. They played chess until one day Harry, too often on the losing end, threw the set out. Wendy was, at the time, a champion badminton player, but with masculine bravado, Harry argued that she didn't have the right winning attitude: "With your attitude, even I could beat you at badminton." Wendy wasn't about to let that go by. She got their small circle of friends to set up a game in the men's gym at a time when the facility was unoccupied. It took some doing. Women were not allowed in the building, so friends stood guard while the game went on. "I beat him 15–0, 15–0, 15–0. He was exhausted and pissed off and furious. He had to win. Losing was not part of his vocabulary."

A late Christmas, January 4, 1963, with Harry in a full leg cast. Wendy had fallen
while wrestling the tree into their apartment before Harry came home from the
hospital on January 3. Deborah Catherine Jerome would be born on January 19.
The City of North Vancouver came to the rescue of the young family, helping them
through a period when they had no income.

"Rejection really hurt him," she said, describing an incident that Harry had shared with her. (I heard the same story from others, including one of his siblings.) When he went to visit his grandmother Edith on Vancouver Island, her second husband, "Happy" Sumpton, wouldn't let him into the house—clearly, to all concerned, on racial grounds. "You can't bring him in here," Happy declared. It wasn't until after Sumpton died that his grandmother felt free to identify publicly with her famous grandson, telling a magazine writer that Harry was like her first husband, Armie Howard. A photograph, taken early in 1963, shows Harry with grandmother Sumpton, his mother, Elsie Jerome, and two of his siblings, Valerie and Louise.

When we are young, we know so little about life and love. Those brought up in a strict family or religious tradition follow the norms of their class and their upbringing, which usually include well-defined roles for males and females. Many never challenge the pressures of their upbringing, staying "within the traces" for life, playing out their traditionally assigned roles, for better or for worse. The lucky ones can build deep, and often pragmatic, relationships. The unlucky ones discover, sometimes years later, after the stardust of courtship and conquest has turned to dust devoid of any glow, that their spouse was never the answer to their dreams.

It's much, much harder for those who grow up with poor role models—fathers and mothers who live a kind of Cold War—who, if they stay together at all, do so "for the sake of the kids," cheating on each other until the situation becomes unsustainable and they go their separate ways, emotionally and spiritually, if not physically. The children of these unions are set adrift in the world, destined to chase idyllic dreams of romance until, in the wake of the sad outcomes of serial monogamy, life wises them up to reality. Some, with maturity that often comes only long after the waves of romantic ardour have subsided, can get lucky and form relationships based upon realistic expectations. But such luck is elusive. Too many end up lonely and disillusioned, finding other ways to bring meaning to their lives.

Harry and Wendy, after a long, up-and-down courtship, were married in Edmonton at Norwood United Church on Saturday, June 30, 1962. Interestingly, it was Lionel Locksley Jones a friend of Wendy's, who had gone to school with her at Edmonton's Victoria Composite High School, who was the best man. Jones is a descendant of one of the first Black families to migrate to Alberta from the U.S., the first Black provincial court judge in Alberta. None of Harry's Vancouver friends was there. A report in the *Edmonton Journal*, under the headline "Harry Does Altar Sprint," said the wedding caught everyone by surprise. "Harry's parents, Mr. and Mrs. Harry V. Jerome, didn't attend the wedding, and his coach, Bill Bowerman, didn't know anything about it." Even Paul Winn, who had advised Harry against the relationship with Wendy, didn't find out until after the fact. But evidence shows that the couple had secretly been making plans for some time. "Do you really want me to go and pick out a diamond ring for myself?" Wendy had written earlier that spring.

The wedding, however, did not play second fiddle to Harry's athletic agenda. He didn't break training. On the Monday after the wedding, Harry competed in the 56th Annual Highland Gathering Track Meet in Edmonton, winning both the 100- and 220-yard dashes on a soggy track after a heavy rain. Wendy had arranged his participation through the popular Edmonton actor Wally McSween, a past president of the Edmonton Highland Games Association. McSween wrote Harry in May:

> Without wishing to offend your modesty I know
> it is safe to say that your presence as a competitor
> would be a guarantee that 1962 would be the best
> ever...so I am authorized by the Edmonton High-
> land Games Association to extend to you our offer
> to pay expenses involved in bringing yourself and
> any two running mates of your choice to Edmonton.

Harry and Wendy spent the first few months of their marriage living in a renovated garage in Eugene, Oregon, while Harry trained for the British Empire Games at the end of November. But Wendy was pregnant, and they wanted the baby, expected in March 1963, to be born in Canada. So, before Harry headed for the Games in Perth, Australia, the couple moved to Vancouver, where the snake of racism again raised its venomous head. An apartment owner refused to rent to them, insisting that, regardless of the still-running ad, there was no vacancy—a situation that proved to be a lie when they urged a couple of their white friends, also apartment hunting, to check out the same building. Their friends ended up renting the very apartment that was not available to the Jeromes. Journalist Brian Pound found out about the incident and wanted to write the story. "I thought he should," Wendy said. "I was surprised, given how well known Harry was, that he didn't want to rock the boat." Pound confirmed that Harry was adamant in his refusal to let the story go public.

The incident surely triggered the by then partially repressed boyhood memories of the petition raised against his family when they first moved to North Vancouver. They must have hit him like a psychological neutron bomb, leaving physical structures intact but destroying emotional life. He had to get the shame of it behind his defensive wall. He had to be ready to compete. His focus on winning gold at the British Empire Games had to fill every waking moment. They finally found accommodation at 275 Garden Drive North, near the Second Narrows Bridge. Paul Winn thought that the apartment owners who refused them were not nearly as sophisticated as others who didn't like racial minorities, those who never told you there was no vacancy, simply quoting a very high rental price that was beyond the means of most applicants and achieving their objective that way.

Such was the frame of mind in which Harry made the long flight to Perth, where he encountered the greatest tragedy and the biggest challenge of his life. After a devastating injury prevented him from finishing the 100-yard sprint, he came home on the first available flight, crushed by the devastating press coverage of his failure.

Wendy and Harry pose for a snap taken in Edmonton soon after they were married. The house in the background is across the street from her parent's home at 116th Avenue and 84th Street.

"If it's a boy, he won't sprint," Wendy said after the Perth Games, speaking about their coming child. "The publicity Harry has received as a runner has been too hard to take," she told a *Vancouver Sun* reporter. With Harry in hospital through Christmas, Wendy tried to make up for it by arranging a celebration when he got home, just after New Years'. Heavy with child, she bought a tree and was wresting it into the apartment when she fell and hurt her back. The child was born after a difficult labour on January 19, two months ahead of schedule. Deborah Catherine Jerome spent two weeks in an incubator before she was discharged from the hospital. But she grew up to be as feisty as her father.

It was a hard time in their lives. Wendy had been forced, in accordance with the policies of the day, to give up her teaching job after the third month of her pregnancy. Harry was immobile. They had no income. And that was when British Columbia's warm, generous face showed itself. The City of North Vancouver passed a resolution to provide financial support for the Jeromes through the dark winter of 1962–63. A letter dated December 19, 1962, from North Vancouver City Clerk R.C. Gibbs was sent to Harry Jerome while he was still a patient in the Centennial Pavilion at the Vancouver General Hospital. Gibbs' son was a contemporary of Harry's, and they had participated in sports events together. The letter advised that a meeting of City Council "of the 17th inst." had approved a series of recommendations that would help the young family through their difficulties: "Would you therefore forward to Mr. William Carmichael, City Treasurer, any medical, hospital or other proper expenses for payment by him." [17]

The North Vancouver Chamber of Commerce added its support, with a letter from Manager J.E. Turnbull stating: "Your outstanding achievements in the international sports world are deeply appreciated by the citizens of the North Vancouver community. As a small token of that appreciation, the Councils of the City and District have agreed to underwrite some of your expenses resulting from the period of enforced inactivity you are now passing through." A scholarship was established in Harry's name.

It was a long way from the "not wanted in the neighbourhood" petition that had greeted the Jeromes when they first moved to North Vancouver. Harry was, in the view of the people of North Van, far from a quitter. The young couple was profoundly moved. "They fed us and paid our rent," Wendy said. "I've never forgotten that. We felt so bad, and so appreciated."

But 1963 was a long, long year. Paul Winn and his new wife Elizabeth came by frequently for dinner and to spend the evening. Once in a while, Harry and Wendy would go out. Other friends and family visited from time to time. But Harry seemed, much of the time, to be retreating into himself as he turned over in his mind, again and again, the terrible events that had taken place in Australia. He couldn't sit still. He hated. He raged against being called a quitter. He was determined to get even. It never occurred to him—he would not entertain the thought—that he might never run competitively again. One important source of support on this issue was Dr. Hec Gillespie, the surgeon who had performed the operation on his leg and had encased his leg in a heavy cast from ankle to hip. The cast stayed on for six months. Harry, unable to drive and pinned down, brooded and plotted his comeback.

Harry and Wendy were dealing with realities completely new to them. Up until this time, there had always been lots of out-of-house activities—Harry's training and competing, Wendy's teaching and coaching. Harry's enforced convalescence was new territory. Poor, in large measure housebound, together 24 hours a day, they got along reasonably well. And there was Deborah. She was a healthy and happy baby—the natural centre of attraction for them and their occasional visitors. Harry seemed pleased and, as far as he could, helped, not minding changing diapers. Little Deborah was the glue that held the family together through an incredibly trying time.

Harry got up on crutches and began his rehabilitation, exercising his good leg and lifting weights. His determination was phenomenal. Getting back on the track was the most important thing—sometimes it seemed like the only thing. By the time the cast came off in June, he had developed a training regime that progressed from walking to jogging to short runs, all the time continuing with weight training.

It's astonishing, by any standards, that by fall, Harry was ready to resume serious training. The couple returned to the University of Oregon after Bowerman announced that he was going to keep Harry on scholarship. Wendy, who had completed her post-graduate degree, found a teaching job in Eugene that would help pay the bills. She was incensed when Bowerman started "niggling" about his support, cutting

Wendy and baby Deborah, who grew up to be just as feisty and fiercely independent as her father

Harry back from a full to a half scholarship. She demanded a full scholarship for her husband, but Bowerman would not relent. "We hated each other," she said. Harry gave in and ran on a half scholarship for the next term. "He worked, and he worked, and he worked. And when he started running good times, the scholarship money came back." Quite a reality check!

The fact that by the end of 1963, Harry was ready to start a credible comeback, is a testament to his near-superhuman determination. On Friday, January 24, 1964, he ran his first competitive race at Toronto's Maple Leaf Gardens, a 50-yard dash. He came fourth but said, "Sure I would like to have done better, but it wasn't too bad after the long layoff."

A month later, on February 28, at an NCAA meet in Portland, Oregon, Harry Jerome equalled the world mark for the 60-yard dash with a time of six seconds. He finished two yards ahead of the field. "It is the greatest comeback in track and field history," Bill Bowerman announced triumphantly. "Jerome is Back" read the headline in the *Vancouver Province*.

There is ample evidence that Wendy and Harry truly loved each other, but the marriage was rocky almost from the start. "I don't think either of us had good role models for marriage," she said. There were family pressures. Neither Harry's father nor his sister Valerie were happy about the marriage. "When Debbie was a little girl, Valerie would only come by when I wasn't there. When Harry was away, his father [by then separated from Elsie and living alone in downtown Vancouver] would call and harass me on the telephone."

Wendy was, at the time, partly because of her marriage to Harry, estranged from some members of her own family. Almost inevitably, the couple had problems with money, of which, unlike today's star athletes, they had very little. A September 1964 bank statement showed a closing balance of $118.46 in their joint account—and that was a good month.

The marriage held through the 1964 Olympics. Harry's "greatest comeback in the history of sports" was certified when he won the bronze medal in the 100-metre race. Wendy, trying to stay close, to be part of his life, had arranged to write a column for the *Vancouver Sun* covering the Tokyo Olympics and accompanied him to Japan. Harry, totally focused on the race and perhaps on the principle of not wanting to be accused of nepotism, refused to give his wife an interview for her newspaper column.

They carried on for a while after Tokyo. Back in Oregon, Harry completed his education, earning a master's degree in physical education. He was back in his groove, competing well, many of his records

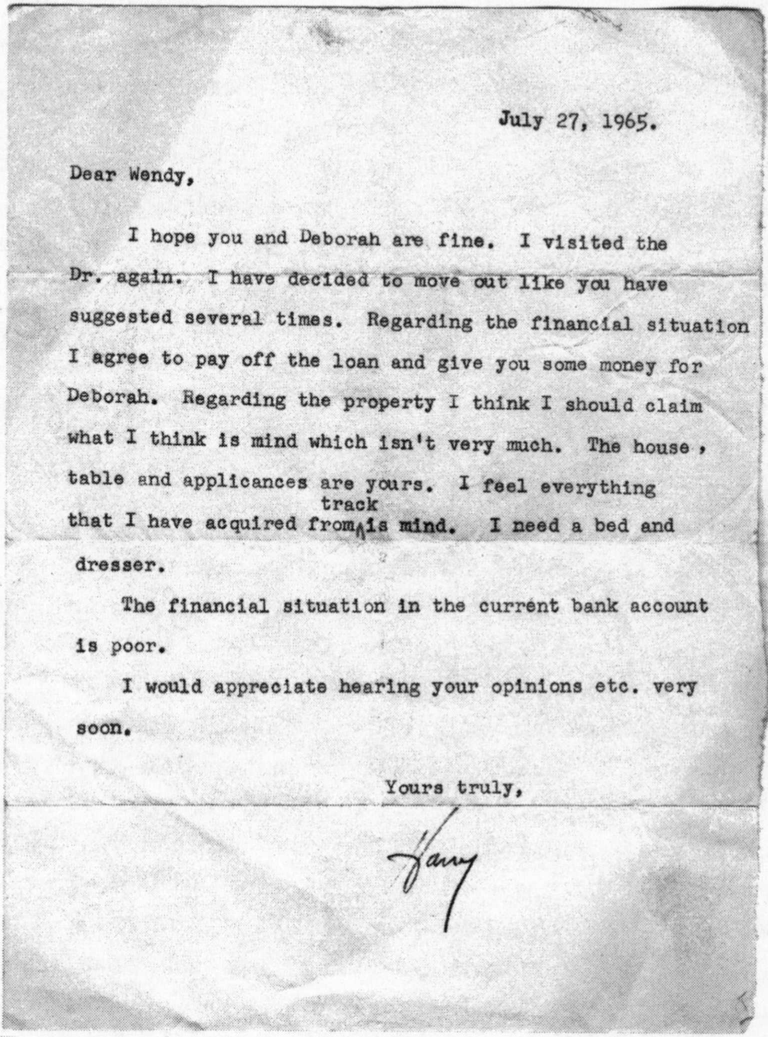

July 27, 1965.

Dear Wendy,

I hope you and Deborah are fine. I visited the Dr. again. I have decided to move out like you have suggested several times. Regarding the financial situation I agree to pay off the loan and give you some money for Deborah. Regarding the property I think I should claim what I think is mind which isn't very much. The house, table and applicances are yours. I feel everything that I have acquired from is mind. I need a bed and dresser.

The financial situation in the current bank account is poor.

I would appreciate hearing your opinions etc. very soon.

Yours truly,

Harry

Harry moves out—it's the end of a marriage punished by external pressures.

still unchallenged. But, finally, the marriage could no longer be sustained. "He was extremely moody and focused. It was hard to share things with him," Wendy said.

On July 27, 1965, Harry wrote: "I have decided to move out like you have suggested several times. Regarding the financial situation, I agree to pay off the loan and give you some money for Deborah. Regarding the property, I think I should claim what I think is mind, which isn't very much. The house, table and appliances are yours. I feel everything that I have acquired from track is mine. I need a bed and dresser. The financial situation in the current bank account is poor."

They tried to get back together a couple of times, but the attempts failed. They finally separated in 1966. Debbie was three years old. Their divorce, given the laws of the day, became final in 1971. I think that, in spite of their troubles, Wendy grieves for him to this day and loves him still. She has kept his name and boxes and boxes of memorabilia that she generously shared with me. She never remarried.

Wendy Jerome completed her doctorate at the University of Alberta and moved to Sudbury, Ontario, in 1969 to take up an academic life from which she retired in 2005. She is recognized as one of the leading sports psychologists in Canada. At Laurentian University, she created the first undergraduate program in sports psychology in Canada. During her tenure, she became a world-class coach. One of her athletes, 17-year-old Margaret Johnson Bailes, whom Wendy had coached since the runner was 11, brought home a gold medal in the 4x100-metre relay in the 1968 Olympics.

Harry, she told me, was a good father who looked out for his daughter as she grew up. Debbie remembers him with mixed emotions. "I only saw him now and then," she recalled, "but he was fun, always interesting." He took her to events and taught her "boy sports," including how to shoot a handgun: "[When he was living in Ottawa] he would take me shooting up the Gatineau Hills when I was 11 or 12. I still have his gun. Once, he got me tickets for Supertramp—backstage

Wendy and baby Debbie cheer as Harry crosses the finish line at a 1964 track meet in Vancouver. "It's my favourite picture," says Debbie.

passes and all. We went horseback riding, and he taught me how to handle a motorcycle." When Harry got interested in horse racing, he would often take Debbie to the track.

But there was a perplexing aspect of Harry's relationship with his daughter. When, as a child, she came to visit him in Vancouver, he always farmed her out to one of his friends. He never let her stay where he lived, even when he and Paul Winn were sharing an apartment. "I think he was afraid of [the responsibility for] taking care of her," Paul said. When Paul was married, Debbie would often stay with him and his wife when she came to Vancouver. On various occasions, she bunked with the Tittlers or the Raders. Al Rader remembers her as quite self-possessed when she was a three- or four-year-old. When they took her to church one Sunday morning, they arrived late and ended up having to sit in one of the front pews (the church typically filled from the back—last in, last out). The congregation sang a closing hymn as they filed out. "Debbie decided if they could sing, she could sing, too," recalled Rader. "She broke into 'We all live in a yellow submarine,' and the place broke up."

Harry didn't mind his daughter being in sports, but not running, definitely not running. It was almost an echo of his father not wanting him to become a sleeping car porter—too hard a life. Debbie was a good athlete in school, but "My father hated me running. He did everything he could to stop me." Debbie, while still in her teens, broke her back in a motorcycle accident. That ended any thought of competing in track and field.

She was a rebellious teenager. She would bleach her hair and wear blue contact lenses. With her café-au-lait complexion, she could pass for a Latino or a southern European or any of the new ethnic groups that were not quite Black and who were becoming a growing and integral part of the Canadian ethnic landscape. She had picked up some Spanish at elementary school in Oregon, where it was a second language, and used it to advantage. She went through many phases of teenage and young adult rebellion. But as a more settled adult, she and her husband live comfortably in Edmonton. She participates annually in the Harry Jerome Awards presentations in Toronto.

Chapter Six

Mixed Media

The earth shook under my feet,
ready to crack open at any moment.
I stopped, trying to steady myself,
and knew for the first time
that I was utterly alone.

–Barack Obama

There's something about sports that inspires intense, often irrational, sometimes frightening fervour. Soccer in Europe, hockey in Canada, football and basketball in the U.S., baseball in Japan, cricket in the East and West Indies and the physically brutal varieties of football played in Australia, can incite fans to terrifying extremes in pursuit of "bragging rights." While sports can build pride in a community or a country, hooligans who wreak mayhem in support of British soccer teams and hockey fans such as those who vandalized Edmonton's Whyte Avenue during the 2006 Stanley Cup playoffs have created chilling models of fandom.

The need to win manifests itself across a wide spectrum. Prior to the 2004 Athens Olympics, a half-page ad in the *Edmonton Journal* sponsored by Bell Canada, "a proud sponsor of the Canadian Olympic team," pictured what looked like a two-year-old boy preparing to lift a huge barbell loaded with 160 kilograms in weights. The headline "Can technology turn him into an Olympian?" raised questions more interesting than, I think, the ad intended. How far will we go? What price are we prepared to pay for victory? How long will it be before some genetic scientist manipulates some unborn kid's genes to create the designer athlete, perfect for the sport of your choice? How soon before the bionic man or woman turns up on the track? Some people, and some countries, have selected and programmed babies from the cradle. Parents, using powers of persuasion and intimidation, too often go to extreme lengths to turn their kids into winners; witness the behaviour of dads in hockey, tennis and other sports (it is usually the fathers—remember tennis star Mary Pierce's father becoming such an embarrassment that he was banned from the courts) looking for reflected glory, and maybe these days, the big paycheques that come if your child reaches the elite level.

In the end, the answer to Bell Canada's question was to be found in an exhibit they toured across the country, an "interactive pavilion giving visitors an inside look at how technology enhances the life of an athlete. Through Bell's innovative technology, a team of virtual trainers guide you through a personalized journey of eight interactive stations."

The 2004 Athens Olympics may well have been the cleanest games since the Cold War. Some 22 athletes in sports from track to boxing to weight lifting were disqualified for drug-related transgressions, the largest number in Olympic history. Greece's pride and joy, former medallists Kostas Kenteris and Katerina Thanou, pulled out of the games after a suspicious motorcycle accident that, they said, prevented them from appearing for a drug test. They were later accused of doping violations. It was an utter shame for the proud residents of the original home of the Olympics, taking the bloom off what was, contrary to some predictions, a successful staging of the event. Officials spun the story as proof that their anti-doping measures were really working.

The history of sport is rife with the stories of young athletes suddenly thrust by their talent and abilities into the blinding spotlight of world attention. Some, like Wayne Gretzky and, in an earlier era, tennis star Arthur Ashe, seemed able to cope, thanks to strong family support, with grace and restraint. Others cover their anxiety with a false bravado that may sustain them for a while. Still others flash across the sports firmament like shooting stars, lighting up the sky for a brief moment before disappearing into obscurity.

In a journalistic lead up to the 2004 Olympics, a July 9 *Globe and Mail* feature by James Christie reviewed a CTV documentary, *Ben Johnson: Drugs and the Quest for Gold*. The article reported that Nike, during the drug-infested sports environment of the late 1970s and early 1980s, had founded a club called Athletics West, based in Eugene, Oregon, home of the international sports conglomerate's founder, Bill Bowerman. The initiative came during an era when U.S. coaches and athletes were seeking ways to "level the playing field" with their competitors from Eastern Europe and other countries where it was more than suspected that the use of drugs to boost the abilities of athletes was routine and sanctioned. The Nike seminars offered information about how steroids worked, how they were most effective and how to avoid testing. There were sarcastic references to East German women who won races and then sang their national anthem in baritone voices.

Poor Ben Johnson was caught right in the middle of it. John Minichiello expressed the opinion that Charlie Francis (Johnson's infamous coach and manager) was not stupid: "In spite of the fact that I don't like his ethics, he's a very brilliant guy, and I'm sure he had it planned as to when to take him [Johnson] off the drugs....I just don't think that Francis would have given him drugs that close to the competition. I think Ben must have taken it on his own, because apparently, you get that sense of confidence with the drugs—you're very aggressive. Maybe he was worried about losing it. But who knows?"

I once saw Ben Johnson sitting in a sports equipment store in Toronto's Eaton Centre during the late 1990s, hired to promote some brand of sports equipment. He was set up at a stand towards the back of the store. No one went near him. People would come into the store, see him and walk out. I went over to talk to him and to wish him well. I remembered the naïve pride and almost childlike bravado of his earlier career. "When the gun go off, the race be over," he would boast. But, alone in the store, ignored even by the staff, he seemed depressed; his answers were monosyllabic. Many athletes felt he had been set up. They felt sorry for him. So did I.

The expectations loaded onto the backs of athletes often follow ethnic or racial lines. Way back in 1910, in the publicity heralding the great prizefight between Jack Johnson, the first Black heavyweight champion, and his opponent, Jim Jeffries, the latter was singled out as the "Great White Hope of the Western World," spotlighting the vast racial divide. Everyone knows how Muhammad Ali shocked America when he embraced Islam. He had the fortitude to face down his detractors, letting his fists do most of the talking—not that his mouth

Two great champions—Harry Jerome and Muhammad Ali

was idle. He was a hero to Harry Jerome, and there are smiling pictures of them together. Ali lived through the condemnation to become an international hero, dramatically carrying America's torch to light the flame at the 1996 Atlanta Olympics. In spite of his impairment by Parkinson's disease, he continues to have a positive impact on the sensibilities and pride of Blacks in America and around the world.

We place gargantuan expectations on the shoulders of elite athletes. The 2006 World Cup of soccer dramatically illustrated how whole countries hitch the star of national pride to their teams, with hundreds of thousands of citizens pouring into the streets to celebrate victory or to agonize over failure. We want—no, we *need*—our athletes to be as close to superhuman as possible. They must not only be physically magnificent. We need them to be mentally tough, able to handle any abuse that comes their way with stoic detachment or, better still, with witty but cutting Ali-style comebacks. We need them to reach heights that the rest of us can aspire to, but never really hope to achieve. Our need for heroes seems to come with being human. We yearn for here-and-now mini-gods, for larger-than-life versions of ourselves. Thanks to modern globe-circling media, both amateur and professional athletes can have their lives and personalities distorted by the adulation and expectations of tens, if not hundreds, of millions of fans and, in this century, by stuff-of-dreams paycheques. So much is at stake that some will, almost inevitably, take whatever risks they need to win and damn the long-term consequences. New revelations about the self-serving management of drug-testing programs, even in the U.S., keep coming to light. Records are cancelled, medals withdrawn, and the asterisk is becoming a common feature of American baseball statistics.

It's absolutely certain that drugs were never part of Harry Jerome's life. But, unlike Muhammad Ali, he had trouble dealing with the celebrity that came so suddenly. He was still a shy teenager, without the skills that allow more mature or self-possessed icons to deal with the klieg lights of celebrity. The creators of fame, the keepers of the flame, the cheerleaders, the judges and jury of athletic prowess are the journalists who talk and write about sports. They thrive on creating heroes, only, with often devastating effects, to drag them down at the slightest misstep. Early in her career, Canadian hurdler Perdita Felicien struggled with the weight of expectation that the sports establishment placed on her young shoulders.

The journalistic emphasis on examining the most private minutia of celebrity's lives, in the name of the "public's right to know" and "freedom of the press," is achieving diminishing returns. Today's stars, with great wealth to go with their celebrity, become increasingly remote, living in hermetic bubbles of protection, their public appearances carefully managed. Athletes, because they are most often young and vulnerable, can suffer devastating effects. Thirteen-year-old Jennifer Capriati burst onto the tennis circuit in 1990, telling an interviewer that the best thing about being a professional player was staying in posh hotels and "having room service." Cute! Her subsequent fall into addiction was dissected and reported in detail. Her rehabilitation and triumphant return was one of the great comeback stories in modern sport—a testament to the grit that made her a great player in the first place.

Harry Jerome, already emotionally scarred in his defenceless adolescence by a world that judged his family by the colour of their skin, found himself suddenly catapulted onto the front pages—the subject of intense national and international scrutiny. When he broke Percy Williams' record for the 200 metres in May 1959, the local and regional press turned the media spotlight on him. But when he equalled the world record for the 100 metres in July 1960, the whole world's press wanted to know everything about this fast Black kid from North Vancouver. The attention was withering. Muhammad Ali, born two years after Harry, was still two years away from his first professional fight against Archie Moore. The great tennis champion Arthur Ashe, born in 1943, was three years away from being the first African American selected to play on the U.S. Davis Cup team. Martin Luther King Jr. was just beginning to be taken seriously in the lead up to his 1963 "I have a dream" speech. The Kennedys were just breaking the surface in their quest for the American presidency. Nelson Mandela was in jail. Pierre Trudeau, almost a decade away from politics, was enjoying his salad days as a rich bachelor. Billie Holiday's 1939 recording of "Strange Fruit" still had a powerful effect on Blacks everywhere. Lynchings were still being performed and celebrated in the American South.

Harry was acutely aware of the way his colour affected the way people saw and treated him. His response was to keep his head down, try to be cool, pretend it didn't matter. At the same time, the fiercely competitive spirit that made him a winner would not allow him to suffer fools or patronizers gladly; his fuse could be very short. He could be uncommunicative, almost sullen, or he could explode with a devastating verbal attack. Those competing traits, like ice and fire, contributed to an adversarial relationship with the sports media that,

Harry in the starting block at the 1966 Commonwealth Games in Jamaica.
There was a gold medal waiting for him 100 yards down the track.

for more than half a decade, frequently escalated into an ugly war of
words.

It is one of the facts of journalism that reporters always check previous dispatches before they write their own stories. That's how attitudes, mistakes and misconceptions, nicknames and labels get carried
from one story to the next. It started with *Vancouver Sun* sports columnist Denny Boyd. When I visited him in his West Vancouver pent-
house apartment, he told me that, even though they eventually became
friends of a sort, he and Jerome got off to a rocky start. "He infuriated
me," Boyd said with considerable passion many years after the fact,
recalling his first column about the 18-year-old phenom. Boyd went
to the Jerome household for the interview, and "Harry ruined the
interview by inviting every teenager in the neighbourhood to sit in."
His report was anything but kind.

It's important to take a careful look at the journalistic record in order to grasp why so many sportswriters were so down on him. The relationship between Jerome and the Canadian sports establishment was, at best, strained and often uncommonly nasty—a caustic connection that profoundly affected his life. The record, particularly in print, is extensive and much of it can be found in the online archives of major newspapers.

Probably the first national reporter to write about Jerome was the *Globe and Mail*'s Scott Young, father of rock star Neil Young.[18] Young made a special trip west to meet Harry at his North Vancouver home shortly after he had achieved the world-record time for the 100 metres. He, and the world, wanted to know who this young "phenom" was and where he came from. Young didn't learn much about the real Harry and ended up describing him as a "yes and no guy" who gave short answers to questions and didn't talk much.

While Young was in the Jerome's house, a radio station team showed up to record an interview with the new "golden boy" of Canadian sports. Harry, casually dressed, was sitting on the piano bench, leaning back (not forward) defensively, trying to parry the questions from the insistent journalists. Young watched as the radio reporters asked a series of written questions, possibly prepared, he thought, at Harry's insistence. As the radio interview began, other members of the family, Carolyn, Valerie, little Louise and their mother, Elsie, drifted into the room. Someone turned on a radio, and Harry suggested that he and the radio guys go outside to do the interview.

Scott Young remained in the house and reported on scattered bits of conversation. Harry's father, Elsie Jerome said, was away a day and two nights at a time. He was then on the CNR Kelowna run. Valerie allowed that her father was not athletic—he was short and fat. She had got into track at about the same time as Harry. They trained in the evening, but not together. And no, they didn't follow any special diet. Elsie said that she was not, herself, athletic, but revealed that her father, John Armstrong (Armie) Howard, was a track star who had represented Canada in the Olympics. "Harry and Valerie are built like my father was," she said.

Later, driving away with one of the radio guys, Young was told that they had used up two tapes trying to get Jerome to talk about what made him go. "He really didn't talk in either of them," the radio man said. "This may cause some to call him aloof." Young wrote later, setting in print (and figuratively in stone) one of the terms that, with variations, would turn up repeatedly in future descriptions of the young athlete's demeanour.

It may have been the last time that journalists were invited into the Jerome home.

The refrain, describing Harry in various ways as "difficult," was picked up time and time again. Toronto columnist Jim Proudfoot, in a year-end column handing out "Proudfoot's Annual Sports Awards," described Jerome as "the sullen, inhospitable Vancouverite who can run faster than anybody else in the world."

It's hard to square the journalists' image of Harry with descriptions from friends and family who knew him best as "shy and self-conscious." He could be "prickly," too, his friends said, and hard to deal with when he felt challenged. Even some of his best friends found him hard to fathom, hard to get close to. The only place where he was truly comfortable was on the track. And even there, he felt he had to prove himself over and over. But the relationship between Jerome and the media had a toxic tone that only began to ease after his comeback success at the Tokyo Olympics. When I talked to journalists such as Alan Fotheringham, Denny Boyd, Brian Pound and others, many said with hindsight that they had, at the time, misunderstood Harry. "I didn't have all of the facts," Fotheringham said when I asked him about the harsh treatment he gave the runner in his initial dispatches following the Perth British Empire and Commonwealth Games in his coverage for the *Vancouver Sun*. Others protested that they didn't write the headlines, which often overemphasized points made in the body of the story. But in my experience as a one-time headline writer,

From left: Harry Jerome, Ed Roberts, Bob Hayes and Dave Blunt, all competitors in an NCAA track meet. This may have been the day after a card game, which became so competitive that, according to journalist Brian Pound, the athletes almost came to blows.

the purpose of the headline is to attract readers to the major thrust of the story, even if it somewhat caricatures the issue.

Harry was among the fastest men in the world, and when he won, the cheerleading media celebrated. He was their Canadian idol. He would show the world. But when he lost, the reaction could be brutal. Syndicated columnist Dick Beddoes was one of the few journalists who, from time to time, stood up for Jerome. In a passionate, almost bitter article published just before Harry departed for the British Empire and Commonwealth Games in Perth, he attacked a feature written by Mac Reynolds in the influential *Toronto Star Weekly*. He described Reynolds as one of the "unlicensed psychologists in search of a journalistic buck" who had taken to analyzing Jerome's performance and behaviour. "They're all amateur head-shrinkers snooping into the dark recesses of his psyche." Reynolds was not alone among journalists who speculated in print as to whether Jerome would "choke" in Perth as he had at the Rome Olympics two years earlier.

Beddoes attacked the fickle reporters and fans, who seemed to want to vicariously share Jerome's successes but not his failures. "They wear their vanity on their sleeves for a team or an athlete, but their vanity is piqued when their guys lose. They turn on the losing players like reptiles gobbling up their own young," he wrote.

Strong words! But old, yellowing copies of the *Vancouver Sun*, the *Globe and Mail*, the *Toronto Sun*, the *Toronto Telegram* and the *Toronto Star*, among others, provide a tawdry record.

Olympic Games, Rome, 1960

The first really big event to bring Jerome to international attention was the 1960 Olympics. Harry's mood was optimistic. "Dear Dad," he wrote from Rome. "Arrived in good shape. The plane ride was smooth. We will have to adapt ourselves to the time. We lost nine hours. The village is nice. We trained tonight. They have eight tracks… perfect for training. The food is pretty good." He was proud that his younger sister Valerie was also on the national Olympic team.

The Toronto media virtually had the gold medal around Harry's neck before the race was run:

- "Vancouver's Jerome Looms as Top Prospect in Olympics," *Toronto Star*, May 16, 1960
- "Canada's Top Sprinter Now," *Toronto Star*, June 1, 1960

- "Harry's One of World's Fastest Men," *Toronto Star*, July 16, 1960

- "They Can't Beat Jerome—He's a World Beater," *Toronto Telegram*, July 16, 1960

- "Harry Jerome Heads Olympic Track Team," *Toronto Star*, July 18, 1960

- "Jerome Best Bet for Gold Medal," *Toronto Telegram*, August 25, 1960

- "Harry 'The Jet' Jerome," *Toronto Telegram*, August 27, 1960: "…the 19-year-old from Vancouver could sprint home with Canada's only gold medal."

The weather in Rome was hot, but Harry, at first, seemed relaxed and confident. It was the most important race in his young career, and he wanted to win for Canada, his patriotism trumping bitter memories of racism. But reporters were everywhere. A self-important Toronto columnist, Andy O'Brien, was "in his face." On the day before he was to run in the qualifying heats, O'Brien insisted that Harry and Valerie hike up to the top of one of the Roman hills for a set of photographs. It was 47°C at noon, Jerome recalled. He was, characteristically, completely focused on his preparations for the race, allowing nothing to distract him. He gave the writer a flat no. He was not there to do the bidding of self-important reporters. The incident stayed fresh in his mind for years and darkened his mood in Rome. O'Brien was furious.

Days later, when Harry pulled up lame in the semifinal heats, O'Brien took his revenge. Writing for the *Toronto Telegram*, he described the "Jerome Flop," a "flopperoo due to what he claimed was a leg spasm." He went on, "The effect of his sheer bad manners towards reporters and photographers as well as Canadian team officials, placed the young Negro down at the bottom as an athletic ambassador for Canada."

It wasn't until four years later, in the run up to the Tokyo Olympics, that Canadians learned the rest of the story behind O'Brien's attack. Jerome, who had kept the story to himself, finally revealed what had happened in an interview with Dick Leutzinger, a writer for the *Oregon Daily Emerald*. "So began the cruel destruction of the image of Canada's most popular amateur athletes," he wrote.

Journalist Brian Pound told me another story about what happened to Jerome on that fateful day in Rome. Harry was late in getting to the stadium for the 100-metre heats because the cab he had taken was caught in a traffic jam, blocks from the stadium. He jumped out and sprinted the rest of the way to the stadium, arriving just as they were calling the athletes for the semifinal. It was a very hot day, and he didn't have time to settle down or to warm up properly before running the heat. Pound was the only journalist who knew the story, but again, Jerome refused to let it go public "until after I win a gold medal." Pound finally wrote the story after Harry won gold at the 1966 Jamaica British Empire and Commonwealth Games.

In spite of all of his training and preparation, Harry was not as ready as he should have been to compete in the semifinal heat before the gold-medal race. He had developed a well-practised routine leading up to his races, isolating himself from everything around him until it was time to settle into the blocks. When the gun fired, he got off to a good start, ahead of the field. But halfway through the race, something went wrong. He grabbed his right leg and, grimacing in pain, stumbled into the infield. Out of the race, he fell to the ground, covering his face. Spectators looked on in surprise and shock. After what seemed a long time, he arose slowly, painfully, and limped his way to the Athletes' Village. When a photographer tried to snap him, he covered his head with a towel. Later, in the first-aid room, tears welling up, he said, "This never happened to me before in a race. Why would it happen to me here? Why?"

Jerome had suffered from a muscle spasm, a tightening of muscle tissues around the bone on his right leg—an injury often referred to at the time as a "charley horse." Dr. Willie Bohn, one of Germany's top specialists in muscle injuries, examined him and confirmed that he had suffered a serious injury. Bohn's presence was neither accidental nor entirely altruistic. German authorities were anxious to stage a series of races between Jerome and Armin Hary, the sprinter with whom he shared the world record for the 100 metres. Bohn thought the injury was serious enough to require a long rest. He even expressed doubts of a complete recovery.

Jerome, meanwhile, was complaining about the treatment he had received from the Canadian trainer accompanying the team, a man from Toronto named Charley Godfrey. He treated the injury with heat and massage, but others who examined Jerome later said that heat was the worst thing that could have been applied. Both a German trainer and an English physician, J. M. Tanner, told Harry that he should have had ice packs applied to his leg as soon as possible. "Canada should send a good trainer and a doctor to the meets," a bitter Jerome complained. "Canada has never had a good trainer to accompany athletes to any international meet." He accused some of the Canadian officials on the team as having just come along for the ride and to help the athletes.

When he failed to win the gold medal for Canada as they had predicted, the sports reporters virtually hung Jerome with the medal's ribbon. The next morning and in the days that followed, some reporters hinted, while others stated outright, that Harry had not suffered an injury but had quit under the strain of competition—unable to compete under the pressure of the big races.

"Canada's Chance for Gold Medal Goes Limp as Jerome Pulls up Lame in Semifinal," shouted the *Toronto Telegram*.

The *Telegram*'s Andy O'Brien led the charge. "Of course, the unpopular Jerome could hardly have expected a sympathetic press anyway," he wrote, going on to question whether Harry had really suffered an injury or had simply lost his nerve. "Luckily, he was the only one of our 99 competitors who failed to win respect."

Another *Telegram* columnist, Ted Reeve, known as "the Groaner," had crafted an image of himself as a professional curmudgeon. He went even further. "Jerome was sulking before he started," wrote Reeve.

"And after the alleged leg ailment, he should have been put on the next boat home."

Other athletes in the village were reported to have shunned Jerome, who retreated to his room and even deeper into himself. The *Telegram's* Milt Dunnell reported that there was "considerable secret rejoicing" over Jerome's failure to finish. He told readers that a Canadian man attending the games had stood up from his seat behind the press row to proclaim that he was happy to see the sprinter's "defeat." "I came to see that guy get licked," Dunnell quoted him. "He got licked good."

Some of the Canadian officials, the report went on, quietly agreed that while the loss was bad for Canada, it might prevent Harry from becoming "an insufferable egotist for the rest of his career in athletics." In his column, Dunnell called on leaders of the Canadian team to tell Jerome that being a sports celebrity carried with it certain responsibilities, among them accommodating people who wanted to meet him and shake his hand. "Now is the time to let him know the score."

Dunnell claimed that Jerome had insulted a well-known but unnamed Canadian magazine writer, telling his wife, who, according to Dunnell, had asked an innocent question in an attempt to make conversation. Jerome supposedly replied, "I don't know who you are, but I came over here to run—not to talk." I wonder if the magazine writer and his wife were "making conversation" in tones similar to that of the man in the stands who was so pleased to see Harry lose. Or was the question just patronizing?

Jerome's attitude, Dunnell told his readers, became the talk of the Canadian's in the Athletes' Village, "Incidents such as this have put the Vancouver sprinter in the position where he has few sympathetic friends at a time when he needs them most. He has been so insolent to so many people that they find it hard to remind themselves that he is young and probably the victim of some bad advice along the way. They would like to see a Canadian win a gold medal, but they prefer to have some person who will make friends for Canada in his role as Olympic champion. Jerome scarcely fills the bill."

Jerome, badly stung, fought back.

"I May Even Quit Canada, Says Irate Jerome," *Toronto Telegram*, September 2, 1960:

> "Who is being an egotist?" he roared in a telephone call from Rome. "Am I being egotistic for wanting to win a gold medal for Canada, or is a magazine writer who is more interested in getting an interview for which he is being paid? Is it more important that I spend my time on interviews or on athletic preparation?"
>
> When told that several Canadians had secretly rejoiced over his defeat, he lost any semblance of cool: "All right, if this is the way they feel about it, I am going to quit Canada and move to the United States, or hang up my running shoes altogether. These insults certainly don't help my mental attitude either. I feel like packing up and leaving right now."

The war of words escalated.

"Harry Jerome Blasts Track Coach, Trainer," *Toronto Telegram*, September 21, 1960:

> "The only way Canada will get gold medals in Olympic competition is to buy them," Jerome said bitterly, arguing that Canada should follow the Europeans and make track and field a business, "just like football, but on an amateur basis."
>
> He called for Canada to offer scholarships to its best athletes, to set up international tours so that they could experience real international competition and to have them train at home for at least a week before travelling. Through it all, Jerome offered no excuse for what had happened. "I was beaten by better runners. It's not their fault that I pulled a muscle.

I could have finished. But I would have had to crawl
on my hands and knees to do it."

The response took the obnoxious hostility to new levels.

"The Boy (Jerome) is Plain Nuts," *Toronto Telegram*, September 21,
1960:

> The injury that put Canada's gold-medal threat
> Harry Jerome out of the recent Rome Olympics was
> diagnosed this morning as a tightening of the head
> muscles—not the leg—by Toronto physiotherapist
> Charles Godfrey. "That *boy*[19] refused treatment to
> start with," shouted a much-riled Godfrey. "He was
> nasty and uncooperative. I think the muscles that
> tightened were the ones in his head....It's just a case
> of sour grapes on Jerome's part," Godfrey was quoted
> as saying. "The *boy* is just plain nuts. Everybody was
> trying their best to help him. He tightened up under
> pressure, and that's all there is to it."

If you can think your way back to the 1960s, when the civil rights
movement was just getting under way and the American South was
a racial war zone, Blacks in Canada, whose country didn't even acknowledge that it had a problem, were especially sensitive to how they were
perceived. Think of the baggage carried by the word "boy" and you
may get some insight into how Harry, whose father and grandfather
had to put up with being called "boy" by passengers on the railroad,
must have been outraged by the incipient denigration carried by the
term. Harry was no boy.

But it went on.

"Jerome Wins One Title, At Least," *Toronto Telegram*, September
21, 1960. Sports Beat columnist Hal Walker crowned Jerome as the
"Olympic Pop-Off Champ."

> He fell flat on his face competitively and left
> thousands of Canadians with a letdown feeling when

the *big* race came up for him. Jerome's only a youngster, of course, but he shouldn't try to cover his own
shortcomings by putting the heat on other people.

Years later, in 1963, Eric Whitehead, writing for the *Vancouver Province* reflected, "Jerome certainly did have a harsh experience in Rome. So harsh that a lesser competitor might never have recovered. The slanderous innuendoes of 'quitter' that followed his sensational collapse in the Olympic dash semifinals with a muscle pull were as cruel as they were unfounded."

Almost overlooked in the coverage was the fact that Jerome, show-ing unexpected determination and grit, did, in fact, compete in the 1960 Olympics, recovering from his injury in time to run in the men's 400-metre relay on September 7, a week after the injury. His team placed second in its heat behind the United States, qualifying for the semifinals. But in the semifinals, the foursome, consisting of Lynn Eves, of Saanichton, BC; George Short, of Saskatoon, Saskatchewan; Terry Tobacco, of Cumberland, BC; and Jerome, came fourth behind Germany (anchored by Armin Hary), Venezuela and Britain. Canada and the United States finished with identical fourth place times of 41.1 seconds.

Armin Hary won the 100-metre race for Germany with a time of 10.2 seconds, short of the record he still shared with Harry Jerome.

The *Toronto Telegram* closed in 1971 because of falling circulation and a lack of advertising. During its heyday, the paper provided the most intense, most opinionated coverage of events. Struggling for survival against the more popular *Toronto Star* and *Globe and Mail*, the *Telegram* leaned heavily, in its headlines and in it columns, towards the sensational. Their reports of Jerome's performance at the Rome Olympics were the worst example of overly inflated, personally vindictive reporting. It should be no surprise that it was key members of the staff of the *Telegram* who would become the creators of the *Toronto Sun*, beginning a trend that has lowered the standards of jour-nalism across the country.

The images set in print were as permanent as if they had been chiselled in granite. In the buildup to the British Empire and Commonwealth Games in Perth, Australia, no matter how often Jerome was lauded for his successes in scores of track meets during the next two years, journalists never let Jerome, or their readers, forget that he had failed them in Rome.

Chapter Seven

"I Tried Too Hard"

*…the only thing you could choose as your own
was withdrawal into a smaller and smaller coil of rage,
until being black meant only the knowledge
of your own powerlessness, of your own defeat.
And the final irony: should you refuse this defeat
and lash out at your captor,
they would have a name for that, too,
a name that would cage you just as good.*

—Barack Obama

In the two years following the Rome Games, Harry Jerome set or equalled records for the 100-yard dash, twice. His 10-second time for the 100 metres still stood as a world record, as did his record of six seconds for the 60-metre bolt. He was the first athlete to simultaneously hold world records for both the 100-metre and 100-yard dashes. He helped set a new record for the 4x100 relay and tied the U.S. NCAA record for the 220-yard run. He remained unchallenged as the Canadian sprint champion, the fastest man in the country.

The *Vancouver Sun*'s Archie MacDonald was practically rhapsodic in a July 23, 1962, column: "A masterpiece by Harry Jerome hangs in the gallery of Canadian track records today. He took the 100-yard dash and gave it power and beauty. He ran it in the [then] record time of 9.3 seconds."

In Edmonton, days after his wedding to Wendy and after competing in the Highland Games, a mellowing Harry said, "It took me a long time to realize it, but one sportswriter's opinion doesn't necessarily concur with that of everyone else in the country. I'd be proud to run for Canada again, and the criticism wouldn't bother me in the least this time."

Jerome was the only Canadian listed in the 1962 world track and field rankings for men. He was training hard and getting advice from technical coaching wizard, Bill Bowerman:

> September 1962
> Dear Harry,
> ...It seems to me you have a little hitch in your
> left arm. If you can straighten or smooth this out,
> making it a smooth, fast arm action as you come off
> the blocks or as you execute a starting manoeuvre,
> I think it will give you a better move. You might also
> experiment with having your hips just a little lower,
> maybe two inches is enough. When you're taking

a workout, don't take full-speed starts, but trot along, drop down into a starting position, come out smoothly and pay considerable attention to that left arm so that it doesn't make that hitch.

I would suggest now that you plan on a fairly good workout every other day. Do a little high knee, a little fast work on this heavy day, then do some starts going about 40 yards, take from 6 to 10 and none of them wide open. Then stride through about four 110s, and you might just as well do these on the turn as on the straightaway. Stride through some-where between a 300 and a 500 and then do some moderate 110s on the grass. Your light day should be just going out doing easy calisthenics. No stretch-ing—that is too much of a strain. On your weight lifting, if you have a set of weights, follow this chart that I have here and don't lift too much of the heavy one. You want to be careful about putting on weight. Watch your eating, watch on your weight lifting that you're not seeing how much you can lift, but build strength through light stuff with repetitions.

Bowerman, rating Jerome as the best 220 sprinter in the world, told *Vancouver Sun* sports reporter Bruce Larsen that when he ironed out the "hitch," Harry could expect to run the 100 yards in 9.1 seconds. It took four years, but Harry, at an age considered old for a sprinter, validated the prediction in 1966.

British Empire and Commonwealth Games, Perth, 1962

The first competition to be named the British Empire Games was held in Hamilton, Ontario, in 1930. The event became the Brit-ish Empire Games and Commonwealth Games in 1954, the British

Commonwealth Games in 1970 and finally assumed the current name of the Commonwealth Games when they were held in Edmonton, Alberta, in 1978.

The 1962 games were held in Perth, Australia, from November 22 to December 1.

While Canadians are hunkering down for the blasts of winter at that time of the year, it is high summer in Australia. The climate in Perth, in the arid southwestern corner of the continent, is characterized by hot, dry summers and rainy winters. The summer of 1962 was exceptionally hot.

The buildup to the 100-yard race was, if anything, even more intense than it had been in Rome.

Some of the coverage was encouraging, if a bit condescending. "Maybe Harry Jerome will be used to the weight on his shoulders when he heads to Australia and the British Empire Games next November," wrote the *Vancouver Sun*'s Bruce Larson.

The Canadian coach for the games, Fred Foot, predicted the Canadians would win at least three medals. "We've got Harry Jerome with a double chance in the sprints, we've got (Bruce) Kidd in the six and one other event, and any one of our three pole vaulters could do it," he said.[20]

There were the usual headlines, practically awarding gold medals to Jerome before the race was run: "Nobody should beat Harry Jerome in the 100 or 200 yards," *Vancouver Sun*, November 9, 1962.

In the run-up to Perth, feature articles about Jerome appeared in two of Canada's most important national magazines, the *Toronto Star Weekly* and *Macleans* magazine. The *Star Weekly* led off with a wounding attack, reminding viewers where Harry had come from; that he was definitely not part of the mainstream. The essay, written by Mac Reynolds, drew angry responses from a few other journalists. "If gold medals were awarded for charm," Reynolds began, "the least likely Canadian competitor at this month's BEG in Perth, Australia, could well be Harry Winston Jerome." Displaying the vanity-driven whinging

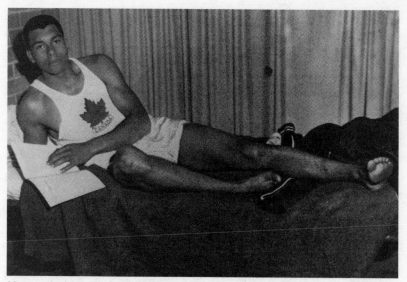

Not as relaxing as it seems. Harry is in Perth, Australia, suffering from a throat infection just before the competition.

of many in the sports establishment, he continued, "He grants news-papermen little time, cooperation or respect, with the result that he suffers from a generally poor press."

Reynolds then crossed a line that would have resulted in complaints to Human Rights Commissions, if not lawsuits, were it written today. He played what would today be described as "the race card," ranting "Defiant of conventions, Jerome, son of a Canadian National sleeping car porter and a white mother[21] who are now separated, was never known to date a Negro girl. When he married in Edmonton last July, it was to a white girl, a school teacher. Except for his 18-year-old sister Valerie, a lithe, handsome girl who's almost as promising in high school track and field as he was, Jerome has deliberately cut himself off from his own family. Even Valerie, devoted to her brother as she is, said recently, 'Harry is very hard to live with. He's thoughtless. He forgets to think about other people. He's the sort who will dawdle for hours in a bathroom while there's a lineup outside.'"

It was a shameful ambush, echoing ancient fears of miscegenation, an assault no mainstream newspaper would allow today. While a few journalists stood up to defend Jerome, one writer tried to excuse Reynolds, arguing that he suffered from "…severe editing. Many of the favourable things he had to say about Jerome were deleted."

Peter Gzowski's piece in *Macleans* was more balanced but could not avoid the references to race. "Jerome has had what a professional actor would call a bad press," he wrote. "In the time I spent with him, he was invariably polite, cooperative and gentlemanly. Coming from a home that is now broken, never well off or outstanding in school, a Negro in a world that does not prepare Negroes for sudden fame, he could hardly have been expected to act like a crown prince."

The flight from Vancouver to Perth is very long, even today. No one has ever survived it without jet lag. But Jerome put on an optimistic face: "I feel in top shape. I have trained myself to a fine edge for these games."

But the facts, revealed in letters home to Wendy, showed that he was a long way from being "in top shape." Using those aerogramme letters of the era with the blue, thin-as-tissue paper, he wrote that he was suffering from what he thought was tonsillitis and was running a very high temperature.

November 23: "My cold is improving, but I still can't talk too well. Today it was 100° [38°C] in the shade. Some places downtown 140° [60°C]. I am feeling thirsty all the time."

Another November 23 letter (he wrote every day, sometimes more than once): "Today I have one hell of a clogged up windpipe. I can hardly talk. I hate flies. The minute you step outside, there are flies all over you."

November 24: "Well, today is the day, great or lousy—I am scared—I feel about the same as my first race against Norton.[22] The temperature will be around 102 [39°C] in the shade and flies. I didn't sleep too well. I coughed most of the night away. When I get home, I'm going to get my chest and throat looked at."

Harry knew that he was not in top form. He was training, doggedly, with a mustard plaster taped to his chest. But he was face to face with the biggest dilemma of his life, the ultimate Catch-22—damned if you do, damned if you don't. If he took himself out of the race, he knew the media would crucify him. If he ran and failed to win, the result would be exactly the same—they would come down on him like a whirlwind. He told himself that he had to go out there, that whatever it took, he had give his all to win.

"They have never let me forget that I was a failure at Rome," he said. "Although I pulled a leg muscle in the preliminary heats, some of my critics led everyone to believe I choked up. It has been a hard dose of medicine for me to take. I must win here, and I must win in the Olympics in Tokyo to get out from under this cloud. ...I feel I must win a medal to prove myself," Jerome said. "My aim is to win the 100, and then I will feel I have got over a hump."

Neither of his coaches, John Minichiello or Bill Bowerman, had they been allowed to be there, would have let him run. The Oregon coach said that if he'd been in charge of Jerome in Perth, he would have scratched him from the 100 in hopes the chest condition would clear up in time for him to run the 220.

But none of that was revealed to, or picked up by, the media. The buildup continued. Alan Fotheringham, writing for the *Vancouver Sun*, was on his way to becoming a journalistic luminary. He was probably the lead Canadian journalist attending the Perth games. His colourful writing style was already evident in a series of dispatches, carried on the paper's front page.

"Jerome to Start in First Heat Perth," *Vancouver Sun,* November 21, 1962:

> They've picked the fastest man in the world to
> be the first to test the vaunted new track in $2 mil-
> lion Perry Lakes Stadium. Unless the world goes

flip-flop and Cuba invades Australia before Friday,
Harry Jerome will be the first man to breast a tape
as the weeding-out of the strays from the Commonwealth's swiftest runners begins. ...One of Jerome's
hazards is the constant pressure and attention of
photographers, reporters and autograph seekers. He
complained that his track work is constantly inter-
rupted. "I don't want to offend anyone but I have to
be able to concentrate on my training." A little more
policing of the track would help.

Sick or not, Jerome managed to excite the crowd when he ran the
first heat of the preliminary round of the 100-yard dash. Reports said
that he never turned on the full power yet was clocked at 9.4 seconds
to tie the Games record.

But the old baggage still clung. This time it was ignited by Jerome's
greatest nemesis among the athletes. While all athletes competed hard
and used anger and hate as motivating weapons during a race, for most
of them, a level of courtesy and respect prevailed between races. Some,
off track, were good friends. The exception, for Harry, was Mike Agostini, a former runner who had retired from the track and was working
as a media commentator at Perth. Agostini had won a gold medal
for Trinidad, running the 100 yards in Vancouver in the 1954 British
Empire and Commonwealth Games. Strangely, he switched allegiance
to Canada and wore Canadian colours in the 1958 games.

Agostini had a reputation as a needler and was proud of it. Talking about how he won the 100-yard dash at the 1954 British Empire
and Commonwealth Games in Vancouver, he said, "My tactics were
simple. I kept asking out loud around that Athletes' Village who this
guy Hec Hogan was, and every time I saw him, I laughed in his face or
giggled at him. He hated my guts by the time we were ready to get into
the starting blocks in the final. Then I leaned over and patted him on
his back and said, 'All the best.' He was completely upset, and I won it
in 9.6. The thing to do is to get the guy hating you. Tactics depend on

the individual. If the guy was moody or temperamental, I'd tap my forehead every time he looked at me. Soon he'd start trying to avoid me, but I'd hunt him out, and by the time the race was ready to go, he wouldn't be prepared. With another guy, I'd build him up and then unexpectedly chop him off with some slurring remark just before the race."

Fotheringham was present when Agostini made what he described as "a slashing attack" on Jerome. "Jerome will not win the 220," Agostini stated flatly. "He may win the 100 yards, but he'll never win the 220. No athlete should be that cocky without having his tongue in his cheek." Agostini loudly announced day after day that Jerome couldn't win the big ones.

And so on, up until race day.

At the gun, Kenya's Seraphino Antao, a runner Jerome had beaten three times that year, was first out of the blocks. Something seemed to happen to Harry at the 50-yard mark. Tom Robinson of the Bahamas caught up and passed him at 70 yards. Jerome quit running and crossed the tape in a slow trot. He was last. He rubbed his left leg, and struggling to hold his head up, jogged slowly back the length of the grandstand in front of the silent stares of some 25,000 spectators. He had to hide, to figure out what had gone so wrong. Trying to get away in his misery, he even had trouble finding the right hallway leading to the dressing room. Fotheringham and another reporter followed Jerome into the bare dressing room. "I don't know," he kept repeating.

"He seemed dazed by it all," Fotheringham wrote.

"I tried so hard, so damn hard. Just when everything was going so well…my training, my school…I thought I was in perfect shape. I was trying to beat Antao. When I saw him ahead, my whole edge went off, and I sort of collapsed. There was no real pain. I just tried too hard. I don't think I pulled a muscle. He [Antao] got off the blocks real fine. There was just him and me. I tried to catch him but just couldn't make it." Jerome said he thought he could have taken a silver medal if he had hung on. "But my whole heart went out. I was aiming only for the gold."

"He didn't make much sense, and he paced the room and shook his head and swung his arms in bewilderment while the two reporters sat silent," Fotheringham wrote. "He tried unsuccessfully to explain what had happened without appearing to make excuses....He talked of a lump in his leg and how he guessed he'd better get some ice on it."

Harry expressed his feelings in a letter to Wendy dated November 25:

> Dear Love,
>   I guess you heard the news. I don't know what
> you think but I lost fair and square—ran out of gas.
> I hope they don't say I quit and I didn't try real
> hard. I am sorry I let some people down. This cold
> has made life pretty miserable. I am going to come
> home as soon as I can. It's very difficult to tell you
> how I feel. ....I am fine, but I am just mad at myself.

Wendy, having heard the news but not knowing the extent of his injury, sent a card that crossed paths somewhere in the international mail service with his aerogramme, explaining that she was having difficulty getting a telephone call through:

> Everyone here wishes you the best, as you know.
> And we are behind you 100 percent. Brian Pound
> has asked me to tell you that come what may, you've
> got one reporter in your corner. Run your best for us
> in the 220. The result doesn't matter.

Harry's sister Valerie, at the time on speaking terms with Wendy, added her own note:

> Go like hell in the 220.

And, the whirlwind was unleashed. The headlines said it all:

- "Harry Pulled Up and Faded": "Jerome, the 22-year-old holder of the world record in the 100, piled up badly after 80 yards and finished sixth and last in 10 seconds flat."

- "Jerome Loses '100'—Kenya Takes Event; Harry Runs Last"
- "Last at Perth. Jerome Folds in '100'"
- "Jerome Folds Again"

Fotheringham's assessment, in a front-page report in the *Vancouver Sun*, led the charge:

> The crowd stared in wonderment at the spec-
> tacle of Harry Jerome falling to pieces with a gold
> medal waiting for him 100 yards away. ...The
> enigma that is Harry Jerome has put a stamp on
> himself that will be almost impossible to shake in
> future international racing. The North Vancouver
> young man who can be so very, very swift one
> moment and so very mixed up the next is now
> labelled for good or for bad as a sprinter who folds
> when the pressure is on.

A few of the athletes piled on. Tom Robinson, who finished second in the race, said, "He folded as soon as I came up on him. I knew
he would. He did the same in Rome."

Another Olympian, Herb McKinley, said sarcastically, "Jerome
will never win a race in international competition like this. He can
win in the States where there is just one race. But here, the pressure
builds up day after day, and he just can't take it."

Agostini took his shot, saying, "Jerome's arrogance is to cover up
for the fact that he is actually a little boy crying in the dark."

But the greatest humiliation came after Jerome agreed to a post-
race press conference. Mike Agostini positioned himself in the front
row of reporters, setting himself up as a kind of television crime show
prosecutor, leading the inquisition: "Would you say you had a pulled
muscle, Harry, like you did in Rome? Why, Harry, did you run so
well in heats and then couldn't do anything against Antao? [23] Do you
think it might have something to do with you being afraid of him?

Your voice seems drawn, Harry. Is that from your 'sore throat' or from the pressure?"

It was, as Fotheringham wrote, a pitiful scene: "After the race, in the quiet dressing room before two silent reporters who could only sit and watch the agony of a man who had just labelled himself with a nasty word, Harry Jerome seemed like a little boy. At first one reporter then the other got up to leave. Jerome could only plead 'I'm sorry, sir, I'm sorry.'"

The race was run on Saturday. But it was Monday before the real story of what had happened began to emerge. Jerome had been left to his own devices for the weekend, actually going for a swim on Sunday. Canadian officials avoided him. He was finally examined by two Perth orthopaedic surgeons who concluded that Jerome had ruptured the rectus femoris muscle on his left leg, eight or 10 centimetres above the kneecap. They recommended an operation within 24 hours. They also said that Jerome might not have felt the effects of the injury immediately and could have run 50 or 60 metres or more before the muscle injury would slow him up. It was recalled that Jerome appeared to quit running at full speed after he had gone nearly 70 metres in the race. This explained why Jerome was at first confused about the extent of his injury and wasn't sure whether he had pulled a muscle.

The rectus femoris muscle is one of the quadriceps muscles. It goes from the hip to the knee and is used to straighten or lift the knee. It's the kicking muscle—the strongest muscle in the upper leg. The main cause of injuries, according to medical journals, is overuse through kicking or explosive movements as in sprint starts. Tearing it was like losing one of the four cylinders in an engine, except that the rectus femoris is the main cylinder, the others performing more of a supporting role. The doctors said that the rupture probably took place as Jerome, putting incredible pressure on his body, blasted out of the starting blocks.

Harry *had* tried too hard.

One of Australian doctors, Dr. George Bedbrook, said, "If this chap doesn't get treatment, he could be out of racing for life. This is urgent."

The doctors also examined Jerome's throat and confirmed that he was suffering from a serious infection. A third specialist, one of England's best-known doctors, Sir Arthur Porritt, was asked to confirm the diagnosis. An internationally famous surgeon in his own right, Porritt was also president of the British Empire and Commonwealth Games Federation. He concurred with the Perth specialist's recommendation for an immediate operation on his leg muscle. Porritt said that if Jerome had stayed to run the 220, his track career could have been ruined. Harry was adamant that he did not want the operation to take place in Australia, he wanted to go home. He left on the first available plane, an Air India flight that left for Sydney shortly after midnight.

Reporters were waiting for Jerome at the Sydney stopover. "I do not understand what happened to me in the final," he explained. "The physiotherapist told me I was all right, and my left thigh was just a little bruised. I felt okay and thought I could run, but I could not. I am still not sure what happened. Halfway through the race I felt as if I'd hit a hole in my lane and bang! I was finished! Perhaps I became run-down without knowing it. One Australian doctor said that it was like I had four cylinders in the leg but only three were working. It's ironic that I couldn't win the biggest race of the year for Canada. I'm sorry I let Canada down. I've run at least 50 times this year and, before Perth, I only lost twice."

Runner Bill Crothers, in a later magazine article,[24] said: "I was there, and you could feel the indent where his muscle was ruptured."

An unsightly question hovered over the controversy. Where were the coaching and training staffs before the race? They should have realized that Jerome was in no condition to compete. And why was Jerome not taken to see a doctor until some 40 hours after his breakdown in the race?

The *Vancouver Sun* reported that Charles Wayland, manager of the Canadian team, was at a rowing event while Jerome was frantically searching for Canadian officials. After the race, it was at least 10 minutes before the first Canadian official, track manager Ken Twigg, arrived to help the injured runner. Twigg's comments over the weekend were not helpful. He told reporters that Jerome was suffering from tonsillitis and was lucky he didn't cross the finish line on a stretcher. He said that the runner was flying home to have his tonsils out. "He was hoarse, coughing and sneezing," said Twigg, "and had to be treated with mustard plasters on his chest all last week."

The British press cabled home stories that Jerome's leg injury had turned out to be tonsillitis.

Meanwhile, track coach Fred Foot was reported to be spending almost all of his time with Bruce Kidd, who won the gold medal in the six-mile race. Foot, reports said, seemed disinterested in Jerome, injured or healthy.

Finally, there was an official statement. The full text of the press release issued by C.H. Wayland, general team manager, following the Perth Games was as follows:

> Canadian officials at the Empire Games have read with deep disappointment certain reports concerning the reasons for Harry Jerome's return to Canada. Many of the reasons given have not been in conformity with the statement which was released by me as general team manager on Monday afternoon, November 26th. The simple facts and full truth about Harry Jerome's return to Canada are the following:
>
> Harry Jerome ran on Saturday, November 24, in the 100 yd. Final Race. He placed sixth. It was apparent before the finish of that race that he was in physical trouble. Immediately following the race, he received a special massage treatment and it was

believed that his muscular trouble would be fully remedied by Monday, when he was to race in the 220 yds. On Monday morning, we became seriously concerned about the condition of his left leg a few inches above the knee. His condition was such that it was decided that he would not compete in the 220 yd. race scheduled for Monday. The Camp Village doctor conducted an examination and decided to call in two of the leading orthopaedic surgeons in Perth. At about noontime on Monday, November 26, we received a written opinion in which the three doctors stated that Jerome had a ruptured Rectus Femoris muscle, which required immediate reparative surgery.

Harry Jerome felt very strongly that if an operation was necessary, it should take place in Canada, close to his family, rather than here in Perth. As we had been advised that there was urgency in this matter, we solicited the advice of Sir Arthur Porritt, President of the British Empire and Commonwealth Games Federation. Not only is he President of the Federation but one of England's leading surgeons. Sir Arthur Porritt examined Jerome at 5:30 PM on Monday, November 26 and concurred with the opinion that there was a ruptured Rectus Femoris. We then discussed with Jerome the question of an immediate operation, but he was determined to return to Vancouver and have the operation performed close to his family. Under the circumstances and at the express request of Harry Jerome, arrangements were made for his immediate departure from Perth. A telegram was sent to his wife and one of the leading orthopaedic surgeons in Vancouver was contacted by phone and advised of Jerome's condition, and arrangements were made to have Jerome met at the airport so that immediate arrangements can be made for his medical and surgical care.

This has been a great disappointment to all Canadians, but as sportsmen, we must be prepared to accept such reverses. Jerome has been, and is still, Canada's star sprinter. It became necessary for Canada to scratch its sprint relay team, but Jerome's fellow athletes and all members of Canada's BEG team completely understand what happens to any athlete who has the misfortune to rupture a muscle, and we all know that Jerome's personal disappointment is even greater than ours.

While Jerome was under my charge as General Team Manager, I found him most cooperative and am assured by the Track and Field coach and Manager that he gave full cooperation in the matter of training and competition.

We are all anxiously awaiting the results of the operation, and Harry Jerome continues to have the good wishes and admiration of the entire team.

If there is any further information required by the Press, Radio or Television, the undersigned shall be pleased to supply such information, as it is essential that the true facts concerning Harry Jerome's withdrawal be clearly stated as otherwise and great and perhaps irrepairable [sic] damage could be done to the reputation of a great international track and field star.

–G.H. Wayland, General Team Manager

At home, reporters did their best to reverse their earlier comments. In truth, many, both fellow athletes and even some journalists, stood up for Jerome at the time. Teammate Bruce Kidd spoke out: "Harry's injury was just one of those things. As for the ridiculous suggestions that Harry had quit during the 100 final, well, the press jumped to conclusions."

"Harry no more quit than a pilot quits when his engine packs up," reported the CBC's Ted Reynolds. There were scores of angry letters to the editor criticizing the attitude taken by the sportswriters, and Jerome received supportive fan mail from across the country.

An editorial in the *Vancouver Province* weighed in:

> Who did Harry Jerome let down through his failure at the British Empire Games? Canada? Well, hardly. What pride are we entitled to claim that can be affected by the performance of this fast boy from North Vancouver? Who's putting Harry Jerome through university? The Americans. Who keeps him in runners' skivvies and glove-leather track shoes? The Americans. Who transports him up and down the U.S. west coast for tune-up races? The Americans. Who has trained him to world-record-holding trim? The Americans. Where on earth is our pride when we borrow back Harry Jerome from the Americans for international competition and try to pass him off as our own product?

Columnist Dick Beddoes of the *Vancouver Sun* entered the fray on November 27, 1962, by responding to comments by well-known sportsman Ted Hunt:

> We must always remember the heights to which Jerome soared. We in Vancouver, in fact in all Canada, have shared in the honour that he has brought to himself. And never forget that we did nothing to help in the muscle-searing preparation for world-class competition. If we are in any way disappointed

Harry running through a warmup at Hayward Field in Oregon. The other runner may be Dave Blunt.

in his performance at the British Empire Games, can we not imagine his terrible frustration that he must be suffering? And what about the jealous little jackals at his heels? They who would eagerly trade places with him are below contempt in their petty criticism. It behooves "hometowners" to remind the outsiders that everyone has their ups and downs. But when excellence is attained, the peaks are higher and therefore the valleys are lower. If Jerome had a bad day in Perth, so what? We will never forget his world records at Saskatoon and Vancouver and will always marvel at any individual, who for however brief an instant, was at some particular things "the best"…

Mrs. Winifred Foster (in real life, Harry's mother-in-law) of Edmonton, sent a letter to the editor:

I don't want to know if there is a Santa Claus.
I want to know what species of a man is a reporter?
Is he a special breed who has earned the prerogative
and the privilege, God-given or otherwise, to crucify
a man publicly?

And, at the end of it all, Jerome agreed to a question-and-answer
session with Dick Beddoes of the *Vancouver Sun* that was published on
November 28, 1962:

> *Beddoes:* The knockers are saying you quit in the
> race. What about that?
> *Jerome:* I don't think it's fair to say I quit, because
> my time of 10 seconds flat was only half a second
> behind Antao's winning time.
> *Beddoes:* Can you describe then, what happened in
> the race?
> *Jerome:* Antao got off the blocks fast, real fast. I still
> had contact with him at 50 yards and tried to catch
> him because I'm normally a strong finisher. But
> when I tried to make a move this time, I went sort of
> bloopy—bloopy with the leg.
> *Beddoes:* You mean you felt the muscle tear at this
> point?
> *Jerome:* No. I tried hard to accelerate and couldn't.
> It felt like a carpet was slipping under me on a tread-
> mill, and I couldn't gain. I was just beat and didn't
> have it on the day. Antao did. He ran a strong race
> against a headwind.
> *Beddoes:* There is a theory that conditions were less
> than ideal for Canadian runners because the climate
> and season were foreign. Is this theory valid?
> *Jerome:* It was mighty hot, something like 104°
> [40°C] in the shade. Some kind of black flies were
> irritating and just hung on you, awful. But the main

disadvantage for me was that my season had been so long. I've been running since early last spring and reached a peak last August. That meant I had to reach another peak for the BEG, and with the cold and all, I didn't quite do it.

Years later, on his 42nd birthday Jerome, his memory perhaps not completely accurate, reflected on his running years in an interview with Jim Kearney, which appeared in the *Vancouver Sun* on September 30, 1982:

After the race, I knew something was missing. There was a dip in the front of my leg you could put your fist in. I went to the infirmary on Sunday, not for my leg, but to get some pills because I thought I had tonsillitis. While I was there, I asked the Canadian team doctor to please look at my leg. He told me to come back in the afternoon. You see, he was a radiologist and athletic injuries weren't really his specialty. When I got back, two Australian doctors were there, and I found out from them what was wrong. I had completely torn the rectus femoris. That's the big muscle in front of the thigh. It's the kicking muscle, the one punters use when they're kicking the football. The doctors wanted to operate right away. I told them no thanks, I'd rather have it done at home. Early Monday morning, I got on a plane and left. That added more fuel. Everyone thought I was ducking out.

Harry was in a no-win situation in Perth. He was clearly not fit to compete. But there's no doubt that he would have been chastised even more viciously for pulling out than he was for pulling up. He took the disastrous but honourable path.

Canada came fifth in the Games, with 31 medals: four gold, 12 silver and 14 bronze.

Chapter Eight

"I"m No Quitter"

*The constant, crippling fear that I didn't belong,
somehow, that unless I dodged and hid
and pretended to be something I wasn't,
I would forever remain as outsider,
with the rest of the world, black and white,
always standing in judgement.*

–Barack Obama

The operation on Jerome's leg took place just in the nick of time. The muscles in his left thigh had already begun to atrophy. He went immediately from the airport to the operating room at Vancouver General Hospital on November 29, four days after the disastrous run in Perth. The then-challenging surgery was performed by Dr. Hector Gillespie. Gillespie was the team doctor for the BC Lions football club and performed the operation free of charge. Harry spent six weeks in hospital and six months in a full-leg cast, with everyone wondering whether he would ever walk normally again, let alone run. For the rest of his life, his left leg was smaller than his right, marked by an 45-centimetre-long scar.

Jerome's personal physician, Dr. H.W. Spencer, said that the quadriceps muscle was sutured and the leg put in a cast. Doctors considered the situation so serious they wouldn't let Harry out of the hospital for Christmas. He came home on January 3, but the cast stayed on for six months. For the rest of his life, Harry always made a point of praising Dr. Gillespie because, when Harry and most other people were wondering if he'd ever run again, "Hector kept me positive. He wiped away all my fears about breaking down again."

Harry started training, slowly and deliberately, as soon as the cast was off. First he learned to walk without crutches, then he jogged and started weight training and, finally, he began to run again. By the end of the summer, he had worked himself into good enough condition to, with a slight limp, run a quarter mile. By the standard of most mortals, his determination was off the scale. He returned to the University of Oregon to prepare for his comeback. "There's no doubt that it [the surgery] was a complete success as far as the leg and muscle are concerned," said Bowerman, as Jerome trained for his first comeback event at the Telegram-Maple Leaf Indoor Games in Toronto on January 20. "Whether he can become as great as sprinter as he was depends on how much time he can put into it." Bowerman added that it was unlikely that Jerome would go "full blast" in Toronto.

The race was over 50 yards. Wearing his inside-out Oregon t-shirt that spelled NOGERO, he placed third in his qualifying heat, with a time of 5.4 seconds. He finished fourth in the final. The winner, Tom Robinson, clocked 5.3 seconds. "It wasn't too bad after the long layoff," Jerome said.

Within a month, Harry was back in winning form. He placed second in a meet in Winnipeg, and on February 28, in Portland, Oregon, he equalled the officially recognized[25] world record for the 60-yard dash, covering the distance in six seconds flat.

"It was a very satisfying race," he said. "I pushed harder off the blocks this time, because I was gaining confidence. I feel great, just great....The leg? It feels real good. I know I can run the 100 now with confidence."

"It is the greatest comeback in track and field history. It was a combination of Jerome's spirit and his doctor's skill that did it," a happy Bill Bowerman rhapsodized. It made Jerome the only runner in memory to share four world records at the same time, the others being the 100 metres, 100 yards and 4x400 relay.

Former sportswriter Bruce Larsen, by then city editor of the *Vancouver Sun*, offered congratulations and some unsolicited advice in a personal letter to Harry dated March 5, 1963:

> Dear Harry,
>
> What you did last Saturday gives you every right to tell a lot of people to go to hell...some newsmen, some critics and even some fellows who cut down on scholarship money.[26] But this comeback proved you've got more mettle in you than any critic can ever muster. The comeback was a tremendous challenge, and I think that the way you handle it can even be a bigger stride. Your 6.0 timing did all the talking you need. Every guy who ever took the

slightest shot at you got it right down his gullet with that time. You're bigger than they are now, Harry. Don't show it, and your triumph is complete. I know you've had a rough path, but it's behind you, and no great savour could come from gloating.

On March 28, Harry ran the first 100-yard dash of his comeback in the Far West Relays, a track-and-field meet involving five American universities. He won in 9.7 seconds, finishing three yards ahead of his nearest competitor.

With a solid string of victories under his belt, the buildup of expectations for Jerome's performance at the 1964 Tokyo Olympics, set for October, was again in high gear. Coach Bill Bowerman, who probably had his own insights into Jerome's potential to overexert himself, and hedging his bets, wrote this advice:

> Dear Harry,
>
> Soon you will be heading for Tokyo. Harry, the big one for you is the 100 metre. I think you already have realized this, and my only suggestion to you is go into it with the idea that you are going to give it your best. Don't comit [sic] yourself or let anyone comit [sic] you to the idea that you have to win that race. No one has to do anything. All you have to do is go in there and do your best and, of course, a lot of us have the utmost confidence that the gold medal is going to be yours.
>
> I am not going to stick your neck out nor mine out by being the kind of prophet that says, "Harry is going to win the 100." However, I have the utmost confidence that you are going to give it your best effort. Dave and I both wish you all the best.
>
> Sincerely,
> W.J. "Bill" Bowerman, Track Coach

The admonition was clear: Don't overdo it.

Bowerman understood that Jerome's problem was not that he was intimidated by major competition, and he was certainly no quitter. His problem, as Harry himself had said, was that he tried too hard. Harry's desire was so great that, both in Rome and in Perth, under far less than ideal conditions, he had overstressed his body coming out of the blocks. In Rome, because of a taxi caught in traffic, he didn't have time to properly prepare for the race. In Perth, he was just plain sick, with a temperature close to 38°C, and had slept badly the night before, constantly coughing. It was because of these circumstances, and the expectations placed upon him, that he overexerted himself. How hard is it for a finely tuned athlete to press so hard that he ruptures a major muscle? I asked Dr. Brian Maraj, a kinesiologist who studies athletic development at the University of Alberta, how much force an athlete would have to exert to rupture a major muscle. "It would take a huge effort," he answered. "Off the scale! Most people couldn't do it if they tried."

As he prepared for Tokyo, Jerome was still dogged by a mostly hostile media. In my research for this book, I found almost every piece of major newspaper coverage, but coverage by the broadcast media, notorious for poor record-keeping, was harder to come by.

A *Vancouver Sun* piece by Ralph Hall gave some indication of the continuing hostility of Canadian sports journalists: "North Vancouver's Harry Jerome garnered many headlines by blasting officials at the recent Canadian Olympic trials [in Montréal]."

However, he was also harpooned by television sportscaster Dick Irvin, who was less than enchanted by Harry's conduct during the meet:

> The conclusion of the Canadian Olympic trials here in Montréal were marked by a blast at officials from sprinter Harry Jerome. The Vancouverite complained that the meet was held for the benefit of officials rather than for the athletes, that the starter was incompetent and that the organization was chaotic

to say the least. Well, here are a few complaints directed at Harry Jerome, who showboated and loafed his way through the entire proceedings. Along with starting a heat in the 100 wearing sunglasses and another wearing his sweatsuit, Jerome strutted around the premises like the greatest thing in track since the invention of the stopwatch. But his worst offence, so far as I was concerned, was that he loafed through his races. Here was a former world-record holder performing before people who had paid to see him run, and he didn't go all out. Afterwards, Jerome said, "What's the use of killing myself and taking away all the fun." Well, Harry old boy, Bruce Kidd and Bill Crothers, who have done more for Canada on the international scene than you can ever hope to do, didn't let the folks down, despite the inferior opposition. Nor did Abby Hoffman, Nancy McCready and others. About Tokyo, Jerome said it will be a matter of mental attitude and luck. Jerome had better have lots of luck, because he certainly doesn't have the mental outlook of a true champion.

There was much more. But by then, the race was the only thing that mattered.

Olympic Games, Tokyo, 1964

October 15 was, auspiciously, a warm, sunny day. The 100-metre final was run exactly according to the book. The leading contestants included Bob Hayes, with whom Jerome shared the record for the 100-yard dash, Cuba's Enrique Figuerola Camue and American Melvin Pender. Hayes was recovering from a leg injury that he had incurred in June. Pender had led the way in the second heat before the final, but tore a rib muscle and left the field on a stretcher. He was advised not to run the in final, but insisted on doing so.

The start of the race was delayed because one of the lanes had been chewed up by a previous race, and the cinders had to be raked. Finally, the trigger was pulled, and the race got off to a clean start. Ten metres out, Hayes, Figuerola and Jerome were well ahead of the pack. Then the pigeon-toed Hayes, strong and muscular, burst ahead of the pack to finish first in 10.0 seconds, equalling the record held by Jerome and Armin Hary. He was two metres ahead at the finish line. Poor Pender finished seventh in a field of eight and, because he let his desire to win trump the advice of his doctors, spent the next three days in hospital.

Jerome and Figuerola finished in a near photo finish—both were officially clocked at 10.2 seconds, but it was the Cuban who was awarded second place.

Harry Jerome and Bill Crothers, shot in Richmond, BC. They are showing their medals from the 1964 Tokyo Olympics.

Harry Jerome had won the bronze medal. Finally, the weight of failure was off his back.

The next day he came close in the 200-metre race, finishing fourth.

"Sprinter Harry Jerome—Canada's Comeback Kid," *Toronto Star,* October 19, 1964:

By Jack Sullivan

> TOKYO (CP) – One of the greatest comeback stories in modern Olympics track history has been written at the National Stadium by Harry Jerome of Vancouver, supposed to be washed up two years ago. Jerome, who has been an inspiration to the Canadian track team the last few days, missed making it for the second time to the medal-winning podium when he was a driving fourth in the men's 200 metres Saturday at the Olympic Games.

But Harry gave Canada its first finalist in the men's furlong (220 yards or 201 metres) since 1936. At the same time, he exploded the myth that he folded under pressure and proved that he could come back after his personal tragedies in the 1960 Olympics and the 1962 British Empire and Commonwealth Games.

Milt Dunnell, who had attacked Jerome when he was at the *Telegram,* was now at the *Toronto Star.* Somewhat chastened, on October 14, he wrote:

> Harry Jerome, one of Canada's most controversial athletes until these games, ended a 32-year famine for Canada in track and field when he won the bronze medal in the 100 metres. No Canadian had won a medal of any kind in track and field at the Olympics since Duncan McNaughton won the high jump in 1932.

A Different Harry Jerome

At the 1960 Olympics in Rome, Jerome was under fire for his surliness and hostility to all who tried to approach him. When he failed to finish in the semifinal of the 100 metres, there was little regret among those who should have been most disturbed. Then came the serious injury at Perth. Here, there has been a different Jerome. He has been relaxed, congenial and popular with other members of the team, as well as a favourite with press, radio and TV. His third-place finish in the 100 metres today represents a win over odds that should have put Jerome out of international competition for good.

There were accolades from fans around the world and from Prime Minister Lester Pearson: "Canada is proud of the determination that has brought you Olympic honours. Congratulations and kind personal regards."

And John Diefenbaker, who knew something about adverse press, sent a telegram saying: "Congratulations to you who have shown great courage in facing difficulties."

British Empire and Commonwealth Games, Jamaica, 1966

Harry Jerome could have hung up his cleats after Tokyo and enjoyed an honourable retirement, but he was still hungry for a gold medal. He set his sights on the next British Empire and Commonwealth Games, slated for Kingston, Jamaica, in 1966.

But in early 1965, Jerome was sending a very different signal. He told *Vancouver Sun* reporter Tony Simnet that he was fed up with Canadian track officials and was considering retirement. He complained that the country's three leading international track organizations, the Olympic, British Commonwealth and Pan American games

Harry Jerome received congratulations from Prime Minister Lester B. Pearson during a 1967 Centennial year event.

associations, were "doing nothing to help the sport." He accused the Commonwealth Games group of wanting athletes to compete in the Jamaica games, but offering little pre-Games support. "For instance," he said, "the BEG group will want athletes for the games in Jamaica next year, but what is it doing to help them prepare for the event? Nothing." He argued in favour of holding more international meets in Canada.

The sacrifice required to stay near the top, he said, "just isn't worthwhile. ....I am losing too much money."

Jerome told an interviewer for the World Student Games in Budapest: "I think it's time I gave up. I intend to do no running at all next year as I do everything for gratis and that hits my pocketbook."

Later, he told *Vancouver Sun* columnist Eric Whitehead: "What I'd like to do is take a year off and then maybe start thinking about the 1968 Olympics." By June 1966, Harry was still undecided about his competitive future. He agreed to compete at the Canadian Championships in Edmonton in July but was still making up his mind about the British Empire and Commonwealth Games in Jamaica in August. He was busy taking his summer course at UBC and was still unhappy about the attitude of Canada's track officials. "If they want these good performances," he said, "they'll have to organize better."

Meanwhile, Jerome's life away from the track was having more downs than ups. His marriage to Wendy was breaking up. Then, at the end of the school term, in June 1965, he learned that he was being dropped from his teaching position at Richmond High School. The school board said it could not keep him on because his temporary teaching certificate had expired. He had been surprised and upset to learn, after completing his master's degree in physical education at the University of Oregon, and after having taught for a year in the American state, that his credentials were not accepted in Canada, that he had to take additional courses. Harry was not pleased. He noted that the Richmond Board had a letter on file from the Department of Education stating that he would be issued a permanent certificate upon successful completion of a summer school course in the philosophy of education.

"Jerome Fastest Human—Vancouver Speedster Equals World 100-Yard Record" was the headline in the *Edmonton Journal* after Jerome dazzled spectators at the 1966 Canadian Track and Field Championships in Edmonton. He was clocked at 9.1 seconds, 10 yards ahead of his competitors, equalling the mark set earlier by Bob Hayes. Hayes had by that time retired from competitive running and was playing professional football for the Dallas Cowboys. And Armin Hary, with whom he still co-held the record for the 100 metres, was also out of the sport. That left Harry as the fastest human in the world. His coach and friend, John Minichiello, called the achievement "the greatest comeback in track and field in this century. It hasn't been easy. It's a difficult thing to do, a thing that has been underrated. I don't think people realize that sometimes with such an injury you can't walk without a cane afterwards."

On July 18, the Canadian British Empire Games Association announced its roster of 34 athletes chosen to attend the games. The list included Harry Jerome.

But he still hadn't committed to the Jamaica games. "I haven't said I would go, and I haven't said I wouldn't," he stated. But Minichiello told reporters that "he has to work out something at UBC before he'll be able to announce a decision."

Disgruntled or not, Jerome did work things out regarding his summer school course at UBC so that he could compete in Jamaica. Columnist Denny Boyd was sent to Kingston to cover the games for the *Vancouver Sun*:

> The story here is the heat, the blinding exhausting heat, the heat that turns the eyes to pinholes, the brain to porridge and the shirt collar to blotting paper….But you have to figure on Vancouver's Harry Jerome to win the 100 yards, the race he won in a world-equalling 9.1 in Edmonton in the Olympic trials. And Harry has to be a better-than-casual choice in the 220.

"Harry's in the Right Mood" was the headline of Boyd's report a few days later: "Dick Harding, the personable manager of the Canadian track and field team, says he likes the mood Harry is in, withdrawn and tense."

The finish to the Jamaica race was agonizing, but sweet. No better description can be found than that of one of Jerome's few journalistic friends.

"Seven Years to a Photo Finish," *Toronto Telegram*, August 8, 1966:
By Brian Pound

KINGSTON, Jamaica – It took Canada's Harry
Jerome 9.4 seconds to win the 100-yard event Saturday night, and 42 minutes for British Empire Games
officials to confirm his victory and hang a gold
medal around his neck. It was a race Jerome
"couldn't lose." In the BE Games trials in Edmonton
last month, he had tied the world record for the
100 yards with a 9.1. Yet he and Tom Robinson of the
Bahamas lunged into the tape at National Stadium
here in a photo finish ahead of Trinidad's Edwin
Roberts. Jerome had been the big favourite before
and had lost. This was one he *had* to win. Jerome and
Robinson were both timed in 9.4. From the press
box, reporters conceded the race to Jerome. On the
field, news photographers swarmed around Robinson, and the many Bahamians in the crowd were
certain Robinson had won. So were some of the
officials. And for those 42 agonizing minutes,
while officials scrutinized the picture with micro-
scopic care, Jerome sweated out the most momen-
tous decision of his athletic life.

Harry stood in a runway leading to the stadium
arm-in-arm with his sister, Mrs. Valerie Parker, also
a sprinter on the Canadian team. Newsmen stood
guard in silence. There was nothing to say as Jerome
stared endlessly at the giant scoreboard. After
15 minutes of tortuous silence, the public address
system broke the vacuum like a jet shattering the
sound barrier. Mrs. Parker grabbed her brother's
arm as they both prepared for the announcement.
"Athletes please report for the first heat of the

women's 440," blared the PA, and Jerome's face con-
torted in frustration and impatience. The crowd
began to chant for the official result of the 100 yards.
The PA asked the crowd for silence. The hush was as
heavy as the humidity. The PA then directed the
crowd's attention to another medal presentation.
Thirty minutes had crawled by. Jerome tried to say
something, but his mouth was so dry only a whisper
emerged. He asked for a soft drink and then spoke,
"I think I won. I'm not certain, though. Another
drink, please."

When the announcement finally was made, the
immobile Jerome suddenly exploded, shooting both
arms in the air, and while Canadians in the stadium
hugged each other in joyous relief, the kid sister
cried. While Jerome waved his hands above his head,
Robinson lowered his head in disappointment. Then
he quickly went over to Jerome and shook his hand...

In truth, Jerome had waited not 42 minutes but
seven years to step on the podium and receive a gold
medal. Although he has been in world class all his
track life, this son of a railway porter had never
before achieved the glory, prestige and personal
satisfaction that comes from victory."

Jerome had become the first Canadian to win the gold medal in
the 100-yard sprint since his idol Percy Williams achieved the mark
in the first British Empire Games in Hamilton, Ontario, in 1930.

Under the headline "Farewell to Rome," in the fall issue of *Sports
Scope*, published by the Royal Canadian Legion in Ottawa, said:

Possibly the greatest personal satisfaction of any
athlete in Jamaica belonged to Harry Jerome. A frus-
trated, humiliated young man for years, he at last
won a gold medal in big-time competition. That

Harry takes the top of the podium at the 1966 Commonwealth Games in Jamaica. Second, in a photo finish, was Tom Robinson of the Bahamas. Edwin Roberts, from Trinidad and Tobago, won the bronze medal.

came early in the Games, on Saturday, August 6, and Harry was so excited he stubbed his toe en route to the victory dais. ...For six years, since he equalled the 100-metre sprint record in the summer of 1960, Harry Jerome had been on the griddle. Canadians expected him to win at best a medal in the Rome Olympics that year. He failed. He was everybody's favourite in the 1962 BE Games in Australia. He finished dead last. ...This year, for the second time in his controversial career, he had started as co-world-record holder in both the 100-yard and 100-metre dashes. And, this time again, he had his detractors—reporters from Australia, England and New Zealand who had watched him in Rome and Perth and who had openly sneered at him. Many of these were around in Kingston that suspense-filled Saturday night when officials looked at the photo-finish picture and decided—42 minutes after the race ended—that Jerome had finally hit the jackpot. He won by inches over Tommy Robinson of the Bahamas in 9.4 seconds, off his world mark of 9.1.

This was one occasion when the clock didn't matter to Jerome. It could have been 10.4 seconds just as long as he made that short walk from the edge of the track to the victory platform. He remembered Rome and Perth. His teammates and Canadians in the stands also remembered. So did those British, Australian and New Zealand sportswriters. They clustered around Jerome in the underground dressing room. Jerome recognized the men who had told him to his face four years ago that he had "quit" but chose to be courteous and patient with them.

No one mentioned Rome or Perth.

"A lot of people have been waiting for this," said Jerome, "including the doctors who operated on me."

But in the 220-yard run on August 2, which Jerome was favoured to win, the bad luck devil that had haunted him throughout his life let him know that it still had one more kick to deliver. The track was wet, and the conditions were affecting footing for all the runners. On advice from fellow Canadian track star Bill Crothers, Harry changed shoes. According to John Minichiello, now coach of the Canadian track team, "Jerome had complained he wasn't getting good footing. Crothers suggested Jerome try the short spikes, which had worked well for him in the heats of the 800-metre run."

Jerome changed to shoes like ballet slippers with spikes three millimetres long. Then, just before the final of the 200 metres, it rained. The rubber-composition track was covered with water. Jerome was off the blocks well, then slipped on the turn, caught his balance and slipped again, jogging home dead last in 31.1 with a strained leg muscle. He pulled up 64 metres into the race and limped across the finish line. After the race, he found himself again in the dressing room being examined by doctors. Dr. Doug Clements announced the diagnosis—Harry had torn the abductor muscle, where the thigh and groin come together in the left leg, the same leg he had injured in Australia. "It doesn't look that bad now," Clements said, but neither did his injury in Perth until the next day." Crothers quietly changed into track shoes with spikes like sharks' teeth, went out and won a second-place silver medal in the 800.

"I'm drained, I'm tired. I really tried out there, but I just didn't have it," Harry said. "All I want now is to take a long rest. I want to keep running and try for a spot on our Olympic team in 1968."

So when Jerome went on to the 1967 Pan American Games in Winnipeg, the pressure was off. One of his old journalistic antagonists, Paul Rimstead, said, "Harry Jerome will soon be 27—ancient for a sprinter—and he has made his comeback complete, no matter what the result this week at Winnipeg in the Pan American Games."

But there were still rough spots in Jerome's relationship with the media. Konrad Tittler, one of Harry's friends, told me the story of an incident that took place at a pre-Games reception. A local sportscaster, Tittler recalled, had said something uncomplimentary about Harry on air. When he walked up to Jerome at the reception and put out his hand, Harry refused to shake it. The man, sputtering with rage, shouted "Jerome, you'd *better* win that race…"

"Revenge on a Rainy Day," *Toronto Telegram*, July 31, 1967
By Paul Dulmage

WINNIPEG – The town is wild about Harry.
Vancouver sprinter Harry Jerome made a wild, des-
perate lunge at a tiny piece of string yesterday, stum-
bling and pitching forward into a pool of water
beyond the 100-metre finish line. When he got to his
feet, he had the finish line trailing from his chest
and Canada's first track and field gold medal in his
possession. ...The Omega Photosprint camera
caught Jerome shoving his right pectoral muscle into
the tape exactly one one-thousandth of a second
ahead of [the American, Willie] Turner. Off balance,
he stumbled and crashed into the surface of the
track, sending up a rooster tail of water deposited by
a shower earlier in the day."

When the official result came, Jerome recalled
he'd "taken a worse spill than that in a hockey
game." The race had been run on a new "Tartan"
track, which turned out to be slippery under wet
conditions. "Nobody should be surprised the way I
fell and splashed at the finish," Harry said. "After all,
I am an Oregon duck."

Then there was the story told to me by *Vancouver Sun* columnist
Denny Boyd. The journalist and the runner had had a prickly relationship; but Boyd, in later years, told me that he had gained Harry's
confidence. According to Boyd, Harry, win or lose, had decided he
would not go to the press room following the race for the traditional
mass-media interview. "I saw him the night before and asked him if
he was going to stiff me, too," Boyd reported. "He said, 'If you're going
to be in the press room with the rest of the vultures, don't wait up for
me. If you want to meet me somewhere else, maybe...'"

"I asked him what he had to suggest. He got this big smile on his face and said, 'Tell you what. It's the end of my season. You get a bottle of gin and meet me in the parking lot behind the stadium. If I win the gold, we'll have a drink and talk.'

"So when the starter's gun went for the final, I hurried out of the stadium through a gate at the finishing end of the race. Harry won and kept running, right out of the same gate, with the finishing tape still wrapped around his chest. We broke open the gin and, leaning against somebody's car, we toasted victory and the good life."

Some of Harry's friends don't believe the story, and it seems at odds with the press reports of the race. But Boyd wrote about the incident in a column following Harry's death in 1982. And I heard it from Boyd's own lips when I visited him in 2005.

The Winnipeg injury had a direct impact on Jerome's performance in the Canadian National Exhibition Centennial International Track and Field meet held in Toronto less than a month later. The *Globe and Mail*'s Ed Waring reported that Harry's performance in the 100-yard dash on August 20 was the major disappointment of the event. Harry was disappointed, too. He took the microphone after the race to apologize for his poor showing.

"I guess I was really afraid to give the leg a real test," he said, explaining that he had injured his left leg—never as strong as his right after the operation—in the Pan Am 200 in Winnipeg. At least this time, there were no snide comments from the press gallery, at least not in print or out loud.

And Jerome still wasn't finished. In the run-up to the 1968 Olympics, he took to wearing a t-shirt with the slogan "You can do it, Charlie Brown" across the front. "Charlie Brown is someone who never grows old," Harry told all questioners. "You can read a lot of things into it."

Olympic Games, Mexico City, 1968

And so, weeks after his 28th birthday, Harry Jerome represented Canada at the Mexico Olympics, running the 100 metres in 10.1, the

Harry Jerome and members of the Cross-Canada Sports Demonstration Tour team, with Prime Minister Pierre Trudeau during the spring of 1970. Harry was the captain of a six-member team that included hurdler and long jumper Michael Mason, gymnasts Diane Shelley and Marilynn Minaker, pole-vault specialist Gerry Moro and javelin thrower and hockey player Bill Heikkila, as well as a general manager Bert Allen, a former CBC Television producer.

same time awarded to three others. Officials placed him seventh, well out of the medals. By the time the Olympics reached Mexico, times were measured in hundredths of a second. Jim Hines won the 100 metres in 9.95 seconds, setting a new Olympic mark. Hines had broken the record held by Jerome and Hary for the first time earlier that summer, on June 20, running the distance in 9.9 seconds at the American Athletic Union Championships at Sacramento, California. It's one of the remarkable facts of track achievement that the 10-second record Jerome and Hary set in 1960 held up for eight years. Jamaican Lennox Miller and American Charlie Green both hit the tape at 10 seconds flat, according to the records, winning silver and bronze respectively.

Pablo Montez, Rogert Bambuk, Melvin Pender and Harry Jerome were all timed at 10.1.

At an impromptu press conference following the run, Jerome announced that his competitive career was over. "I've won a medal in all the big meets. I don't think there's anything more for me to do as a runner. Now I'm going to get involved in amateur sport in another way. I'd like to contribute in a bigger way. We need regional gymnastics and track and field programs....There's a need for exercise, a need for activity."

As Winston Churchill, whose name had been given to Harry Winston Jerome, might have said, "Some quitter!"

Chapter Nine

The Fastest Man in History?

...a handful of black men,
mostly gym rats and has-beens,
would teach me an attitude that didn't
just have to do with the sport.
That respect came from what you did
and not who your daddy was.

–Barack Obama

In the eight years since 1960, when Harry matched the world record for the 100-metre race at 10.0 seconds, much had changed in the rarefied world of sprinting. Athletes no longer ran on cinder tracks; the shoes they wore, part of Bill Bowerman's legacy, were greatly improved; and the athletic world knew a great deal more about training and nutrition. What is astonishing is that Harry Jerome's Mexico time was just one-tenth of a second over the world-record mark he had equalled when he was 19 years old. It makes you wonder how Jerome would compare with other great sprinters. If you could create a level playing field and stage a race that included the fastest runners in the modern Olympics, how would he stack up? It would be a mythical sprint.

Harry Jerome ran on cinder tracks, not today's rebounding, speed-enhancing composite surfaces. He ran with shoes that were primitive compared to today's super-light, scientifically engineered footwear. There was little financial support—no endorsements, no elite training programs or technology. He was a careful eater, but he lived on an ordinary diet. There were no performance enhancers, no "nutraceuticals," the unregulated supplements sold today in some body-building supply stores that can sometimes contain "banned substances."

For today's elite athletes, running is a carefully monitored, full-time occupation, with computerized diets and training regimes. Scientists at places such as the Olympic Oval in Calgary use the latest digital technology to perform rigorous experimental studies to determine the postures, the equipment and the environments that will allow athletes to achieve their best performances. With finely tuned nutrition and training regimes, with precisely engineered surfaces and hi-tech equipment, with coaching practices informed by the scientifically sophisticated fields of kinesiology and human propulsion studies, as well as the latest insights of sports psychology, it's interesting to speculate first,

172 ~ Running Uphill

whether Jerome, in today's environment, might have avoided the debilitating injuries that twice threatened to end his running career, and second, where he would place if he were competing in the 21st century.

In a sport in which success or failure is now measured in hundredths of a second, what if we could turn the apples and oranges of different competitive environments into that elusive level playing field, at least in a virtual world? If we could use today's technology to virtually bring together some of the world's fastest sprinters, could experts handicap a race between Percy Williams, Harry Jerome, his great rival Bob Hayes and some of the best contemporary sprinters? Who might win? What times might they post? Such a mythical contest would be one of the great races of all time, "virtually" matching the Miracle Mile in which Roger Bannister broke through the psychological barrier that said that no man could run a mile in under four minutes.

In search of answers to these questions, I consulted two experts: Dr. Brian Maraj, Associate Dean (Research) at the Faculty of Physical Education and Recreation at the University of Alberta, and Dr. Ruth S. Morey-Sorrentino, Adjunct Assistant Professor at the Faculty of Kinesiology at the University of Calgary.

Dr. Maraj has been a professor of kinesiology at Louisiana State University in Baton Rouge and at the University of Colorado in Boulder. He earned his master's degree from the University of Western Ontario, where he majored in physical education specializing in coaching and received his PhD in kinesiology from the University of Waterloo. As an undergraduate student at McMaster University in Hamilton, Ontario, he competed in the 400-metre hurdles. In 1983, he became the youngest track and field head coach in Canada, heading up the teams at York University in Toronto. His teams won two national championships, the first to win both men's and women's titles in the same year. Four athletes from his teams—Mark McKoy, Desai Williams, Molly Killingbeck and Dave Reid—went on to become Olympians.

At the Commonwealth Games in Jamaica, Harry wins one of the pre-final heats, breaking the tape just ahead of Jamaican runner Lennox Miller.

At the University of Alberta in Edmonton, he teaches courses in motor development and motor learning/control. In his research, he studies the relationship between vision and locomotion and is currently involved in an examination of the effect of auditory stimulus intensities on reaction times. In another stream of his research, he has received national and international research grants to investigate ways in which children with Down syndrome can more effectively learn motor skills. He has won four teaching awards and was recently awarded a McCalla professorship for innovative integration of teaching and research at the University of Alberta.

Dr. Ruth Morey-Sorrentino is one of the scientists who conducted studies at the Olympic Oval, a high-tech facility in Calgary, Alberta, that is a legacy of the profitable 1988 Winter Olympics. She is an adjunct assistant professor in the Faculty of Kinesiology at the University of Calgary and has a PhD in the areas of motor learning and educational technology. Her background includes a bachelor's degree in physical education and sports pedagogy, the science behind how children learn motor skills. Her own athletic pursuits include swimming, in which she excelled at competitive levels, and dance. She studied ballet from the age of 3 to 17. Anyone who knows about ballet dancers will tell you that they are among the most finely tuned of athletes, developing formidable flexibility and strength. I once stood in the wings of a stage on which the National Ballet of Canada, starring Karen Kane, was performing. The audience, on the other side of the footlights and across the orchestra pit, could only see the graceful, seemingly lighter-than-air moves of the dancers. From the wings, I could hear the grunts, feel the jolts and smell the sweat as they performed.

In 2000, Morey-Sorrentino was hired to work with speed skaters and their coaches at the Olympic Oval. She taught them how to use video cameras and new computer software programs to analyze their performance. She worked with world champions such as Jeremy Wotherspoon and Catriona LeMay Doan. In preparation for the 2000 Olympics, she took them to the wind tunnel in Ottawa to test different types of skin suits.

Both Maraj and Morey-Sorrentino are at the cutting edge of scientific developments in their field. I asked for their help in trying to understand what makes some athletes so much more successful than others. And I asked them if we could create that virtual "Miracle Sprint." Their answer was a careful yes.

What Maraj and Morey-Sorrentino told me was fascinating. Our conversations led to the development of a television documentary, in which both will be featured, on the impact of technology on sport.

Video clips of some of the great races by the world's best runners are analyzed in the program. One of the highlights is a computer-simulated race between Canadian stars Percy Williams, Harry Jerome and Donovan Bailey as part of a field of eight of the world's greatest runners.

According to Brian Maraj, Harry Jerome actually ran faster when he finished seventh at the 1968 Mexico Olympics, clocking 100 metres in 10.10 seconds, than when he equalled the world record for the distance at 10 seconds flat in Saskatoon in 1960.

When we sat down to talk in his office in the University of Alberta's landmark Butterdome sports centre, the conversation was a primer on the influence of technology on sports. He stated that there were a number of things to be considered when looking at Harry Jerome's times in 1960 and in 1968. A key difference was that 1968 was the first Olympic Games in which fully automatic timing was utilized.

Before automatic timing, a timer stood at the finish line with a stopwatch, starting the watch when he heard the gun go off. Later, timers were advised to start their watches when they saw the puff of smoke from the starting pistol—light travels faster than sound, so there was some gain in accuracy. There was probably little difference in hand timing between the era in which Percy Williams was running and when Harry started his career. So there is no doubt that Jerome was a lot faster than the 10.8 time Williams logged in the 1928 Olympics, or even the 10.3 he ran in 1930.

And, Maraj said, "Nobody's ever really explored the officials' side of timing races. You've got a gun at the start, and you have people at the finish line with stopwatches. Prior to the introduction of fully automatic timing, human error could certainly play a role."

The reflexes of the timers, their perception of when a runner crossed the finish line, were all subject to human variables. Today, measurements are so accurate that it has been determined that the runner closest to the gun can get a head start that might be measured in microseconds, but in a race that lasts less than 10 seconds, it is a distinct advantage. "Now," he said, "even the loudness of the sound

A muscular Harry Jerome, late in his career, brings home the baton.

of the gun has been measured to have an impact." A close race might depend on which lane you are running in.

"Jerome's time in 1968 was 10.10," Maraj said. "In 1960, his 10.00 flat was hand timed. What we do now with typical hand times—and this is pretty standard—is to convert it to a fully automatic timing by adding 0.24 seconds. So Harry's time from 1960, if you want to compare it to 1968, would be comparing 10.24 to 10.10."

So Harry was faster in 1968 than in 1960. "No question in my mind," said Maraj. "He was."

How do you explain that? A number of technological factors come into play. First of all, the running surface in Mexico was a modern composite, "mondo" surface, designed to rebound to the impact of the runners' feet—giving some energy back with each stride. Cinder tracks absorb the impact of the runners' feet, giving nothing back, in fact, probably slowing them down. Heavier runners, who would pound their feet deeper into the surface, were at a disadvantage. Lighter runners, such as Percy Williams, would fare better. If runners compete on concrete, there is no absorption of the forces generated as their feet hit the surface. If they run on surfaces that are either too hard or too soft or spongy, they cannot perform at their optimum level. But modern tracks are engineered so that the resistance of the surface produces something like a trampoline effect, transferring some energy back to the runner with every step.

Secondly, shoe technology changed dramatically in the eight years between Jerome's first record and his run in Mexico. Shoes were lighter, provided better support and aided in the transfer of energy. They're still changing, as manufacturers such as Nike, Adidas, Puma and others vie to get elite athletes to wear their brands. A particular shoe can result in a measurable percentage increase in a runner's performance. Vincent Matthews, the 1972 Olympic gold medallist in the 400 metres, in his book *My Race be Won*, writes about the "shoe wars" that were going on at the time. There was a huge dispute between Adi Dassler, founder of Adidas, and his brother Rudolph, who founded

Puma. Both were suspected of paying athletes "under the table" to wear their shoes.

There's also no doubt that the training regime Harry used to prepare for the Mexico games was more sophisticated, better balanced than anything he might have been doing as a high school athlete. And then there was the altitude. The higher you are, the thinner the air, and so, with less wind resistance, you'll be faster in Mexico City at 2250 metres above sea level than in Saskatoon at about 480 metres. All of these factors can, to some extent, be quantified.

But, in the end, there is one factor that no one can quantify. "Sometimes there's no accounting for the heart of a lion," said Maraj. "It's impossible to document what it is that makes someone hungry for a particular thing in track and field, getting a record and going after it. There's the magnificent objectivity of track and field, of running because you have a measurable something that you can chase, and I think that serves as a huge motivator. Couple that with somebody who's as competitive as Harry Jerome—and talented—then you don't need any other kind of conditions for somebody to be stimulated enough to go after something like that."

Maraj also acknowledged that coaching, more art than science, is a huge factor. "A really good coach has to have an intimate knowledge of what it takes to get the most out of a particular person—and [Harry's coach] Bowerman had that. If you look physiologically at people who are lining up in the final of an Olympic event today, everybody's pretty much even—but what is it that makes an Asafa Powell[27] go to 9.77 as opposed to somebody else? The difference is probably in the coaching. I think that what Bowerman was doing with Harry was finding the thing that makes him tick—tapping into that internal resource that he had to bring the very best of this man out on the track.

"To be a great coach, you have to have what I call a 'technical eye,' to be able to pick things up."

"So," I said, "Bowerman tells Harry to start with his hips a little lower—'two inches would be enough.' He tells him that if he also paid attention to what he described as a 'hitch' in his left arm, that he'd be able to run the 100 yards in 9.1 seconds. And he does it!"

"That's the art and science of it." Maraj said.

And then there's muscle type. There are two basic types of fibres in human muscles. There are "slow-twitch fibres" and "fast-twitch fibres" (also described as oxidative fibres). Slow-twitch fibres can utilize oxygen more efficiently; they're more resistant to fatigue. Fast-twitch fibres are not as resistant to fatigue, but they can produce a tremendous amount of force. Everybody's got a different combination of slow- and fast-twitch fibres. Sprinters would have a preponderance—as much as 80/20—of fast-twitch muscle fibres; long-distance runners would have the opposite. There are no records of any analysis of Jerome's muscle structure—the technology did not exist during his career—but it seems clear that the muscles in his legs would have been mostly of the fast-twitch variety.

It's possible now to take a biopsy of an athlete's muscles and determine the ratio of fast- to slow-twitch fibres. I speculated with both scientists about the use of such technology. Could coaches selecting their track teams demand biopsies to test for fibre type? Could governments, or their national track organizations, take biopsies and do other tests on children to determine their athletic potential? It was clear to my consultants that something like that was going on behind the old Iron Curtain, where countries such as East Germany and Romania produced athletes that seemed almost superhuman. Programs in those countries and others selected children as young as five years old for occupational streams that included a variety of sports. For example, East Germany produced female swimmers with extraordinary upper-body development.

"If you look at a five-year-old's morphology," said Morey-Sorrentino, "you can figure out what kind of adult they'll be. That's how the Eastern Bloc used to pick their athletes—Nadia Comaneci was absolutely in that category. But this is frowned upon in the western world." She was adamant in arguing that the proper goal should be to develop all-round athletes and pointed out some notable examples of athletes who have moved from one sport to another. Alberta's Cindy Klassen, who, at Turin in 2006 became the first Canadian to win four medals in a single Winter Olympic games, was a hockey player before she became a speed skater. She tried out for the women's Olympic hockey team in 1997. Hockey, at the time, was her passion, her sport. She was disillusioned when she didn't make the team and finally decided to switch to speed skating, with phenomenal results. Another Canadian athlete, Clara Hughes, who skates with Klassen, was a cyclist who won medals at the Summer Olympics long before she switched over to speed skating.

Elite athletics today have become something that Harry Jerome would not have recognized. Running today can be a well-paid occupation. Until his downfall, Ben Johnson lived a rich lifestyle. And any shortcut to fame and money is, as the world knows, too much for some to resist. Maraj and Morey-Sorrentino, in addition to being scientists, are also fans—true lovers of sports. Each has a strong ethical sense that wrestles with questions of where to draw the line between performance-enhancing technology and practices and substances that can give an athlete an advantage. Is sleeping in a low-oxygen tent prior to competing in an event held at high altitude cheating? No, says Morey-Sorrentino. It just saves the time and expense of having the athlete go to the site of the event for advance training. At the Olympic Oval in Calgary, she created virtual environments that allowed athletes to experience the venues in which they would actually perform. Skaters could work out in a simulation of the Salt Lake City Olympic Oval. They could hear the noise of the crowd, could see what the arena would look like and build a mental picture of the environment long before the event took place. "Some people think that's not fair," she said. On the other hand, blood doping—taking blood out of the body and then reinserting it before a race, thereby increasing the supply of blood (there are no drugs involved)—is, for her, on the wrong side of the line.

Eighteen-year-old Harry in August 1959 in an early competition at Hayward Field in Oregon. By the time he was 20, he had become the star of Bill Bowerman's legendary University of Oregon track team, the Oregon Ducks.

Still, as new technologies, new regimes and new substances emerge, it becomes harder and harder to draw the line. The World Anti-Doping Agency has entered the debate about low-oxygen tents, suggesting it might outlaw their use. Archers can take beta blockers that slow down the heart rate, allowing them to train themselves to shoot between heartbeats.

"On the other hand," said Maraj, "if I go out and drink three Diet Cokes before I go out and run my race, then I've got all the caffeine

I need in my system—but it's not over the limit that will test positive. Am I walking an ethical tightrope? Some take bicarbonate of soda to try to neutralize the lactic acids that build up in your body as you're running. You get diarrhea, but you don't care. What these questions test is the moral fibre of people."

And then there's the influence of the media—the unreal expectations and the quick condemnation when you lose.

Hurdles specialist Perdida Felicien is almost a modern-day reflection of the challenges faced by Harry Jerome. The expectations placed upon her young shoulders in the run-up to the 2004 Summer Olympics were overwhelming. Like Harry, she must have believed that her whole future was riding on that race. She came out of the blocks so fast, according to Maraj (who used to run hurdles himself), that she got ahead of herself—suddenly finding herself too close to the first hurdle—and couldn't make the adjustment to clear the barrier.

"That whole race is about rhythm—the entire race is rhythmic. You have eight strides to the first hurdle, three steps between them and then your run in. It's that simple. In the 100-metre hurdles that Perdida runs, you can make those calculations—it's so incredibly structured that you almost have to hold yourself back from being too aggressive."

"She tried too hard," he said.

Just like Harry.

I asked Dr. Wendy Jerome, Harry's former wife and a sports expert in her own right, how she thought Harry would perform today on that mythical "level playing field." Wendy is recognized as a leading sports psychologist. In 2005, after 36 years, she retired from the School of Human Kinetics at Laurentian University, where she established the first Canadian undergraduate program in sports psychology.

"You are asking a difficult question given all the variables involved in running 100 metres," she wrote. "Given the technical advances that were actually begun in sprinting about the time Harry was running (Bowerman's lighter shoes that lasted only a meet or two; power

weight lifting, which John Minichiello advocated, a better understanding of nutrition and supplements, all-weather tracks, improved
starting blocks, etc.) that he did not really gain full advantage from,
the vastly improved financial support for the top athletes, and the
belief that the majority of good times run in the past 35 years were
drug-assisted and not that much faster, would certain encourage his
supporters to believe that he would have been able to beat (or at least
tie) the recent record holders, all other factors being equal. In terms of
the motivations of more recent athletes, I would find it hard to believe
that they were more motivated than Harry. He came back from a hor-
rendous injury to run again. However, the current crop is willing to
risk permanent health problems to succeed. The motivations may be
different, but are they less dominant?"

So how can we handicap different runners from different eras and
create something approaching a level playing field? Drs. Maraj and
Morey-Sorrentino said that it is possible to calculate the percentage
differences between performing with different equipment, on different tracks and under different conditions. Morey-Sorrentino referred
to a study by Stefanyshyn and Nigg that looked at the effect of carbon
insoles in shoes that produced positive results. The shoes resulted in
a measurable one percent improvement in sprinting performance.

With film footage of all of the great runners available, including
Percy Williams, Maraj, Morey-Sorrentino and others could use video
and computer technology to determine the efficiency of each runner's
style, and then put them on the same track, under the same conditions, each with the latest equipment.

In the starting blocks are Canadians Percy Williams, Donovan
Bailey, Harry Jerome, current world-record holder Asafa Powell, Bob
Hayes, Jim Hines, Jesse Owens and Hazley Crawford, who set the fast-
est time at sea level during the 1976 Olympics.

Dr. Maraj first developed a system on paper to handicap this field
of exceptional sprinters. He took into account all the factors that
modern sports science can rate, including the impact of changes in

timing procedures, environment, footwear, track surfaces, coaching, diet, training, physiology, nutritional supplements and the impact of serious injuries. See Appendix I, page 222, for details of his work.

Maraj factored in all the known variables to create a virtual level playing field. There was only one thing that Maraj wasn't able to quantify—heart.

The winner of this mythical sprint should be recognized as the fastest man in the world—ever.

And the winner, at least in this virtual race: Harry Jerome, arguably the fastest man in history.

Chapter Ten

Beyond
the Track

*Away from my mother,
from my grandparents,
I was engaged in a fitful
interior struggle.*
–Barack Obama

The life of a sprinter is usually relatively short compared to competitors in many other sports. You need strong lungs, strong legs, a strong mind and, most of all, a strong emotional heart to compete at world-class levels. Many athletes peak in their teens, when they're still psychologically bulletproof. By the time they are in their mid-20s, like Tiger Woods, the tennis playing Williams sisters, Jennifer Capriati and others, they become mortal. They can be prone to injury, their game can fall apart when they, and their fans, least expect it. Not Harry Jerome. He seemed to get better as he got older. He ran the 100 in 10.0 seconds when he was 19, and ran it in 10.1 in Mexico almost nine years later. He achieved his world-record time for the 100-yard dash when he was 26, a record that would stand for eight years.

And as he grew older, Jerome became increasingly self-assured. He began, cautiously at first, to come out of his shell. A video clip you can find online in the CBC archives captures Lloyd Robertson interviewing Jerome about the famous/infamous Black Power salute at the 1968 Mexico Olympics. Harry, speaking in a low-key manner, confirms his support for the Black Power movement's goals, but muses that he would have preferred it had they found a different way to express them. While he does not say so explicitly, you get the impression that he wasn't happy about seeing sports used for political purposes.

Harry Jerome hung up his spikes—at least so far as international competitive running was concerned—after the Mexico Olympics. He still participated in exhibition events, and, in fact, as a stunt, once raced a horse at the Hastings Park Race Track. They gave Harry a nine-metre head start. He lost—so they named the horse after him.

Jerome's last race was in 1969, when he hastily slipped into running gear and whipped the quickest sprinters in the country at the Canadian national championships. He was 29.

Harry Jerome and members of the Cross-Canada Sports Demonstration Tour team group in team blazers meet Opposition leader Robert Stanfield at the House of Commons.

He had offers to play professional sports. Friends say he could have done well in soccer or baseball. Rogers Lehew, general manager of the Calgary Stampeders of the Western Football Conference, said, "I wrote Jerome a letter asking him if he was interested in playing football." The BC Lions offered him a $5000 contract, but Harry wasn't interested. He had a Master of Science degree in physical education and years of teaching experience.

Jerome maintained publicly, even late in his life, that his colour was "never a hang-up." Not an unusual statement for a person of colour living his life in the white world. It's part of the emotional armour. Yet in later years, he became an increasingly effective spokesman for minority groups—Blacks and, interestingly, aboriginal youth.

He worked quietly in the background most of the time, but he made things happen.

He telephoned the CEO of Woodward's, then a major department store chain operating in western Canada. Because of his well-recognized name, he was put through to the top executive, C.N. "Chunky" Woodward. "How come," Harry asked, "you have a store in downtown Vancouver, close to Chinatown, where a significant portion of Vancouver's Chinese population and your customers live, and yet I never see a Chinese face in any of your ads or catalogues?" Woodward got the message. The very next catalogue began to use non-white models, and Harry ended up on Wooword's Christmas card list. Harry even, for a time, did advocacy work for the firm. The initiative was repeated with Eaton's and with the Hudson's Bay Company.

He was an early supporter of campaigns against smoking. The January 1965 Canadian Cancer Society of BC provincial newsletter features an article on Harry in which he warns students against smoking. "Proper health education to make students aware of the need for care of their bodies should go a long way towards reducing the incidence of smoking in schools," he said.

Harry became a bona fide activist, pressuring governments on many fronts. In June 1979, he and Paul Winn appeared before the Canadian Radio-Television and Telecommunications Commission (CRTC) calling for a better reflection of Canada's ethnic minorities in broadcasting. It was quite a departure from the low-key approach he took when he argued that colour was not an issue. The lack of minority representation on Canadian radio and television, Jerome said, was tantamount to "media genocide." Noting that 40 to 44 percent of school children in Vancouver have English as a second language, he said that there was "a lack of positive role models on Canadian programs for them to identify with." He told them that visible minorities were reluctant to participate in media-training courses because they didn't see themselves in the media "and they feel there is no opportunity for them to break in." Adrienne Clarkson and David Suzuki,

Harry received the Order of Canada from Governor General Roland Michener in 1971, becoming an Officer of the Order of Canada "in recognition of his achievements in track and field events in Canada and abroad and for his services to fitness in Canada."

he pointed out, were the only "upfront, across-Canada people" who were members of minority groups. "The CRTC should be concerned with this lack and with the impact on these visible minorities," he said.

And as he got older, Jerome was becoming increasingly effective in his activist activities. On June 16, 1982, just months before Harry's passing, Jim Fleming, the federal Minister of State for Multiculturalism replied to a letter from Harry:

> Thank you for your letter of May 3, expressing your concern about the under-representation of visible minorities in the Canadian media. I was most interested to receive your thoughtful comments on this matter, and I can assure you that the issue is currently a special priority of the multiculturalism program of the federal government.

Celebrity meets celebrity. Harry Jerome exchanges pleasantries—and maybe a joke—with Bob Hope.

There is no doubt that a longer life would have led Jerome to become a powerful national advocate in the fight for minority rights. With his friend, Paul Winn, a past chair of the board of the Canadian Race Relations Foundation and, for a time, its acting executive director, he would have become increasingly influential.

But other parts of Harry's life, particularly his romantic life, were complex. When he was competing, nothing was allowed to interfere with his training and his life as an athlete. But his fame and good looks made him what we would today call a "chick magnet." He had lots of girlfriends. He'd bring them around to visit his friends, almost as if he was seeking their opinion or approval, at the same time checking out how they would fit in. There were live-in relationships, one of which helps deepen our insight into part of his character. Harry had a two-year relationship with a UBC student I'll call "Jane." They met at a Simon Fraser University dance not long after Harry had won the gold medal at the 1966 Jamaica Commonwealth Games. She was 19, he almost 26. The relationship lasted until the 1968 Mexico Olympics.

Jane described him as reticent, wary of the media, worried about saying the wrong thing. She thought he got more respect in Oregon, where he'd completed his master's degree. He kept in touch with his father, by then living alone in a poor district in Vancouver and drinking, she told me, and saw a lot of his sister Valerie. He brought his brother, Barton, down for Christmas one year "because he felt he needed to," but she sensed that he was uncomfortable with him.

Their breakup was terrible. It was clear to me, 35 years later, that she was still shaken. "I loved him very much. He just stopped phoning from Mexico. He didn't contact me when he got home, and then he told me our relationship was over. He said he'd done something terrible that he didn't want to tell me about." By then she had completed a degree in education and had started teaching but, she said, she was in a state of depression for most of the next year. They would cross paths off and on, but never talked. "There was no closure."

Harry had inherited the male trait of being unable to discuss his feelings. He feared intimacy. Better, safer, to walk away from situations with which you could not cope, rationalizing that it was easier on the other party to avoid ugly arguments, to just say nothing.

Jane still had, and shared with me, a lot of Harry Jerome memorabilia—newspaper clippings, photos, souvenirs of track meets and other events.

Soon after the breakup, Harry was invited by Prime Minister Pierre Trudeau to help set a new national sports agenda. He moved to Ottawa to create a series of programs for Sports Canada. I found a copy of what we would today call his CV (see Appendix IV, page 230). His primary interest was to encourage "utilizing the sports aspect of recreation as promotional, educational and informational means" to involve all citizens but "particularly youth." His first task was to help research ways in which young Canadians could improve their levels of fitness. He participated in an extensive study that led to a February 1969 Department of National Health and Welfare "Task Force Report on Sport for Canadians." Its 58 recommendations included two, most likely inspired by Jerome, that suggested:

a) The Government retain a corps of outstanding athletes and coaches as resource people; and

b) The Government provide grants to establish a series of travelling clinics involving outstanding coaches and athletes.

The result was the first "Cross-Canada Sports Demonstration Tour," sent across the country by federal Minister of Health and Welfare John Munro "to motivate young Canadians towards an active involvement in sports and recreation programs." Harry was the captain of a six-member team of elite athletes that included hurdler and long jumper Michael Mason, gymnasts Diane Shelley and Marilynn Minaker, pole-vault specialist Gerry Moro and javelin thrower and hockey player Bill Heikkila, as well as a general manager Bert Allen, a former CBC Television producer.

Harry Jerome speaking with students during the 1969 Cross-Canada Sports Demonstration Tour.

The tour, which focused on personal interaction between students and the touring athletes, began in the spring of 1970 and, over a period of 10 months, reached 250 senior and elementary schools. The events took place during school hours, and attendance in the school gymnasium was compulsory. The tour received good press coverage as it travelled to such diverse parts of Canada as Sault St. Marie, Hamilton, Trois-Rivières, Ottawa, Winnipeg, Brandon, Québec City, Louiseville, Vernon and North Bay. Adidas was among 25 sponsors who contributed more than $100,000 to the project.

After the tour, Harry came up with the idea for a series of books aimed at young potential athletes, designed to help them learn the rudiments of various sports. The books were published in English by McClelland and Stewart and in French by Beauchemin Ltée. as part of the *Sports Canada Sports Starter Library*. They feature a cartoon character, a "hep" cat named Grunion, described as "a fairly timid-type feline (unlike his great-uncle-twice-removed Leo)" who takes readers through the origins of various sports with the aim of turning kids from spectators into players. Harry Jerome, briefcase in hand, "the guy from the Department of Health and Welfare Canada," appears as a cartoon character in the introductory volume, telling Grunion, "We've embarked on a unique national sports education program, and we think you can help us."

Four of the Grunion books were published in 1973, an introductory volume as well as books on soccer, hockey and basketball. Further volumes on volleyball, gymnastics and track and field were in the works. Hardcover editions were published for schools and libraries, while softcover versions were available to the public at the subsidized price of $1.95. The Department promoted the books through "Fitness Award Mailers"—125,000 of them were distributed to schools, libraries, sports, recreation and youth groups as well as to educators across the country. Over 130,000 posters were distributed and displayed in post offices. Grunion appeared at the 1973 Canada Summer Games in New Westminster and Burnaby, BC, entertaining the crowds with gymnastic and trampoline exhibitions and leading the closing day ceremonial parade.

There were ambitious plans, including the production of a French- and English-language half-hour animated film and the creation of a special "Olympics" volume to be distributed at the 1976 Games in Montréal. Jerome was clearly a driving force behind the program.

"We think physical fitness is important for people of all ages and that sports are fun and a good way to keep healthy," he said. "If children discover this at an early age, they're more likely to carry on with more sports throughout their lives."

Harry's daughter Debbie, who lives in Edmonton, cherishes her copy of volume three of the Grunion series, on basketball, which is specifically dedicated to Harry Jerome. He sent it to her when she was 10 years old. It's signed "Aug. 7/73 Love, Dad."

But Jerome was not comfortable with life and bureaucracy in Ottawa. One report says that he resigned after the federal government refused to follow through with a public-private partnership he had worked out with Kellogg's Canada to promote youth participation in sports. At the end of the day, his interests were in working at the base of the pyramid, not at the top. And he yearned to be back in BC, where he had friends and supporters and could live in a more familiar environment. Unless you're really part of the establishment, Ottawa, though physically beautiful, is not Canada's friendliest city; it is a two-tier society—those who are part of the political and government culture, and everybody else.

He made the move in 1975. One of his first assignments in BC came from the provincial government. Provincial Secretary Grace M. McCarthy wrote him on April 21, 1976:

> I wish to thank you for accepting the assignment
> to examine the effectiveness and viability of the
> delivery systems of recreation, sport and physical
> fitness in British Columbia.

His mandate was to examine each major organization and branch in the field of recreational sport and to make recommendations. As a Research Officer 5, he was paid $1958 per month, or $23,496 annually, and his travel was restricted to the province of BC.

The letter called for an interim report by Tuesday, June 15, 1976.

The major result of this work was the creation of the British Columbia Premier's Sports Awards program, which Jerome developed and, as program director, ran. The program was designed to upgrade the overall level of physical activity in elementary schools. As he had done in Ottawa, he led the creation of a series of handbooks on sports designed for instructors. He and his friend Wilf Wedman shared the editing duties of books on soccer, ice skating, softball, volleyball, field hockey, orienteering, gymnastics and, of course, track and field. The books were funded by the Province of British Columbia and published in 1980. Each carried a message from Harry W. Jerome,

Program Director, thanking a wide variety of British Columbia and Canadian amateur sports organizations, as well as government departments, teachers and school district administrators that had supported the project. The books were a testament to Jerome's broad range of connections with athletes in amateur sports and to his ability to involve them in projects that mattered to him. Their support echoed Al Rader's earlier willingness to go out in the night rain with his starting pistol and stopwatch to help Harry practise his starts.

The preface to each of the books, penned by Harry, read:

> The eyes are bright and intent. The face is
> flushed and beaming with joy and satisfaction.
> There is a glow of achievement, involvement and
> confidence. This is the look the Premier's Sports
> Awards Program seeks to help all young British
> Columbians acquire. It's one we hope they will also
> possess years later as physically active healthy adults.

Ambitious? Idealistic? An impossible dream?

The program is still alive and thriving. In the 21st century, the Premier's Sports Awards Program is a physical education resource program designed to help teachers and community instructors teach children ages 8 to 14 basic sport skills. Developed and administered by JW Sporta (the JW stands for Jerome and Wedman), a professional sports-training organization created by Harry Jerome and Wilf Wedman, the program consists of three components: teaching manuals, skill posters and skill crests. They have become a model of inclusiveness, open to disabled and aboriginal students as well as everyone else. Every year, 1200 schools, 2500 teachers and community instructors and 75,000 children are involved in the program. More than one million British Columbia children have earned sports skill crests.

Quite a legacy!

Chapter Eleven

Sudden Death, No Overtime

Behind me, Billie was on her last song.
I picked up the refrain, humming a few bars.
Beneath the layers of hurt, beneath the ragged laughter,
I heard a willingness to endure.
Endure—and make music that wasn't there before.

–Barack Obama

It's one of the great ironic tragedies in the history of Canadian track and field that our country's two supreme sprinters died, both unexpectedly, within days of each other. Their deaths are linked by a relationship that was made close by careers that saw both triumph and bitter failure, both lives marked by an uneven relationship with the media. Percy Williams was Harry Jerome's hero and friend. Although they did not appear to have spent a great deal of time together, Jerome and Williams shared both a high level of mutual respect and an innate understanding of the challenges each of them faced.

Percy Williams may have been Canada's most unusual running star. Compared to most athletes, he was small. At a glance, some would have considered him scrawny—only 165 centimetres tall and weighing 57 kilograms. Born in Vancouver on May 19, 1908, he was raised by his mother after she and her husband separated when Percy was still quite young. As a child, he suffered, according to some records, from rheumatic fever, which may have left him with a damaged heart. But another report says that he was paralyzed by "bulbar" polio and was not expected to be able to walk. His mother, determined to overcome misfortune, massaged his legs every day. Remarkably, according to a letter from family friend F. Hawkins, Percy fully recovered the use of his legs but "his left arm was slightly withered and created an almost imperceptible lean to the side when he ran."

He discovered, as a high school student, that he could run—very fast. But like Harry Jerome, Percy Williams had to work for a living. There were no sponsorships; there was no government support and, in his era, there were no scholarships. He worked at the Vancouver post office by day and trained at night. In the summer of 1928, he hitchhiked from Vancouver to Hamilton to compete in the Olympic trials. After he made the team, he wrote, "I can't quite understand yet, but they say winning the 100 metres puts me on the boat to Amsterdam."

At the same time, he learned that there was no funding for his coach, Bob Granger—who had taken him on after seeing him run as an 18-year-old at a high school track meet in Vancouver—to accompany him. Percy's mother and others raised money to cover some of the costs, and Granger worked his way across the Atlantic on a cattle boat, arriving in time to administer his then-controversial training techniques to the young athlete. He prepared Williams for the race, not by working him out on the track, but by keeping him warm and wrapping him in blankets. Just before the race, he gave him a coconut-butter massage.

Percy Williams stunned the world, winning gold medals in the 1928 Olympics in both the 100-metre and 200-metre sprint events, with times of 10.8 and 22 seconds. In Canada, the adulation from his country, and the media, was unprecedented. Williams sailed home from Amsterdam to boundless accolades. His mother was sent to greet him when the ship docked in Québec City. They took the train to Montréal, where legendary Mayor Camillien Houde presented him with a gold watch and urged him to "stay Canadian." In Toronto, thousands cheered him at the Canadian National Exhibition; Hamilton presented him with a silver tea service and a gold key to the city; and Winnipeg celebrated "Percy Williams Day," presenting him with a bronze statue and a silver cup. Home in Vancouver, bands played "Hail the Conquering Hero," school was let out for the day, and the city presented him first with $14,500 for his education and then with a brand-new, blue Graham-Page coupe—in its time, just about the hottest thing on four wheels. It was a fitting gift for the hottest creature on two legs.

But the hero worship for Williams—as it was later for Jerome—was short-lived. The Olympic win led to his first encounter with media hostility. The U.S. track world, and especially the American sports press, pooh-poohed his performance, dismissing it as "a fluke." To prove their point, they invited Williams to compete against the top American runners in a series of 21 indoor track meets in various parts of the United States. In the so-called "Iron Guts Tour," running different distances on surfaces ranging from concrete to wooden boards to a horse-racing track, Williams won 19 of the 21 races. In one race with a close finish against the American star, Frank Wykoff, headlines accused him of "stealing the race."

Williams had one more great triumph on the track, in the run-up to the first British Empire Games held in Hamilton, Ontario. In the August 1930 trials in Toronto, he set a new world record of 10.3 seconds for the 100 metres. But then tragedy struck Williams, one that eerily foreshadowed Harry Jerome's heartbreaking experience. On a cold, rainy afternoon in the 100-yard BEG race for the medals, he was 55 metres down the track when he tore a big muscle in his thigh, but he had enough momentum to keep going and won the race. There was no doctor with the Canadian team, and no one seemed interested in having the damage properly examined. Williams was bitter when he recounted the story of a medical exam before he went to compete in the 1932 Olympics in Los Angeles.

"The doctor told me that an operation right after the injury would have repaired the damage completely. But it was too late at this point." After he was eliminated in the qualifying heat in Los Angeles, there was no parade, no reception and no fanfare when he came home to Vancouver. The Los Angeles Olympics was his last meet. Williams never again attended a track meet, not even as a spectator.

Nevertheless, thanks to Harry Jerome and his friends, the Percy Williams Invitational Indoor Track Meet was inaugurated in Vancouver on February 20, 1965. Al Rader, executive director of the Vancouver Olympic Club, was in charge of transportation, radio and TV. John Minichiello was the track referee.

Williams was a reluctant hero. He did not seek public acclaim; he insisted on his privacy and was uncomfortable in the media spotlight. His relationship with the press was on the frozen side of cool, and he made a point of staying away from reporters. His life became an unfolding tragedy. Williams lived with his mother until she passed away in 1977, at the age of 90. He lived alone for the rest of his life, suffering increasingly debilitating pain from arthritis. He never married. He ran a small general insurance business, and his only recreations seemed to be golf and hunting. He was the only athlete to decline an invitation from Mayor Jean Drapeau for living gold medallists to attend the 1976 Olympics in Montréal. In 1979, he was made an officer of the Order of Canada.

November 29, 1982, a grim, grey Vancouver day punctuated by showers—depressed and finally beaten by the bone-deep, unrelenting pain of arthritis in his knees and ankles, Percy Williams took his hunting shotgun out of its case and painfully climbed into the bathtub of his West End apartment. He put the muzzle to his throat and pulled the trigger. He was 74.

Eight days later—it isn't raining, but the clouds are still low over Vancouver; the temperature has barely reached 5°C. In a car negotiating the heavy afternoon traffic on Vancouver's Lion's Gate Bridge, two occupants are quietly, solemnly, discussing Percy Williams' death and memorial service. The passenger is Harry Jerome. He was in the hospital when the news of the suicide hit him like a shockwave, shaking him to his very core. He had checked himself in on November 28, worried about his own health problems. A series of violent seizures had been plaguing him with increasing frequency over the past year and a half. Some of the attacks were so bone-shakingly violent that he would lose consciousness, once dislocating his shoulder. "Where was I?" he would ask when he came to. "I was scared of them," he told John Minichiello.

There was never a clear diagnosis of the cause of the seizures. He had been hospitalized before, but this time doctors were trying—once and for all—to find a clear diagnosis. Their efforts ended when Harry got the news about Williams' death. He checked himself out.

Vancouver Sun columnist Archie McDonald talked with Jerome at the Williams memorial service. "He mentioned the joyless fate which followed the lonely Williams and a couple of other Olympians. His tone...was foreboding."

Earlier that day, Harry had lunched at Umberto's Seafood Restaurant, in an old house under the Granville Bridge, with Paul Winn, Al Rader and Wilf Wedman, his business partner in JW Sporta and a former high jumper who had worked with him at Sport BC. After lunch, Winn went on to another appointment, agreeing to meet Harry for lunch on Thursday. Jerome, Rader and Wedman went on to another meeting in Harry's office at the Premier's Sports Awards program, which included Brian Pound. They talked about creating a major track-and-field event to be named for Williams and discussed future plans to advance the cause of amateur athletics.

When the meeting ended, Pound and the others waved goodbye as Jerome climbed into Judy Strongman's car. With seizures threatening to erupt at any time, he had given up driving. Judy, the wife of politician Gerry Strongman, was also part of his tight circle of friends. The couple had supported many of Harry's initiatives, and he often visited them. Now, after the ordeal of Williams' suicide, he had accepted their invitation to spend a few days out of the limelight at their home, high in the upper hills of North Vancouver. Traffic on the Lion's Gate Bridge, never undemanding on this arc of steel and concrete, was building. They finally made it across and turned right onto Marine Drive, passing the seemingly endless strip malls that line the thoroughfare. Signs of the season were everywhere. As they proceeded up Lonsdale Street, Christmas lights were flashing—blink, blink, blink—their pulses almost hypnotic. Looking at the lights, Jerome appeared to freeze, and then, without warning, his body began to thrash about, ravaged by one of the unpredictable, unexplained seizures. Strongman, a former nurse, had to think quickly. Should she stop the car and try to control the bigger, stronger Jerome? She made a snap decision and burned rubber to reach North Vancouver's Lion's Gate Hospital, just minutes away. But it was too late. Jerome was dead on arrival. He was 42.

Paul Winn, grief-stricken and overwhelmed, cried and cried. The calls fanned out. Brian Pound received a phone call from another Jerome friend, Jack Brockman. "I don't believe it, I just saw him."

Another friend, sports broadcaster J. Paul McConnell, confirmed the news, "It's already on the wire." Pound was asked to handle media relations—and did. He told me that he had driven Harry to the hospital on a number of occasions.

"In spite of all the modern medical technology available to us," Harry's personal physician, Dr. Peter Grantham told the media, "we had not succeeded in developing a definitive diagnosis." He said that Harry did not have epilepsy, though there is evidence that other members of the family were affected by that condition. Nor was there any evidence of a brain tumour or brain hemorrhage. He was a moderate drinker, a healthy eater and didn't smoke. BC Coroner Gerald Tilley said that the cause of Jerome's death was "asphyxia due to aspiration of stomach contents." In more graphic terms, Harry drowned in his own vomit.

Harry's suffering had been a matter of public concern. The BC Minister of Consumer and Corporate Affairs had written him in October 1981, expressing concern that Harry had spent some time in hospital. "Sucha Gill has kept me informed about your progress, and I am pleased to learn that present prospects are far more optimistic than the initial worries....All of us need the usually active and resourceful Harry Jerome in the field—and the sooner, the better!"

Journalist Denny Boyd, writing about Jerome's passing, told a story of how Ted Hunt, a fellow athlete, cherished a gold Longines watch Harry had given him. It was the watch Jerome had won for beating Bob Hayes in the 1962 Modesta Relays 100-yard final. "It said so on the back," Hunt explained. "Harry gave it to me when I was teaching at Templeton High. He'd been helping me with the kids there for three years, and when he was leaving, he came up and said, 'Here, I want you to have this.' It wasn't until after he walked away that I realized how much that watch represented."

A tiny death notice, in six-point type, was placed in the Vancouver papers by Harry's sister Valerie, who unilaterally assumed responsibility for the funeral arrangements:

> JEROME—Harry, passed away suddenly
> December 7, 1982, at 42 years of age. Survived by his
> mother, Elsie Ellen Jerome, sisters Carolyn and Louise
> Jerome and Valerie Parker of Vancouver, brother
> Barton of Kelowna, daughter Debra of Sudbury,
> grandmother Edith Sumpton of Sidney, nieces Leslie
> and Andrea Jerome, nephew Stuart Parker. Memo-
> rial service at the Unitarian Church, 49th and Oak,
> Saturday, December 11 at 2:30 PM, Phillip Hewitt
> officiating. In lieu of flowers, donations to the Harry
> Jerome Scholarship Fund, c/o Vancouver Founda-
> tion, 1199 W. Pender, Vancouver. Arrangements
> through the Memorial Society of BC and First
> Memorial Services.

But the newspapers covered the event with front page stories.

The memorial service attracted more than 350 people. Paul Winn, Al Rader, John Minichiello, Wilf Wedman, Dr. Hector Gillespie and singer Leon Bibb paid tribute to their friend. Senator Ray Perrault, swimmer Elaine Tanner, past chairman of the Canadian Olympic Association Harold Wright, BC cabinet members Stephen Rogers, Grace McCarthy, Jim Nielsen and Allan Williams and the Tittlers, as well as his mother and siblings, were all in attendance.

There was a small, private funeral for family and close friends. But in a strange twist, unexplained to this day, when the family arrived to the gravesite to pay their last respects and to inter Harry's body, they discovered that the casket was already in the ground, the grave already filled in. Harry's sister Valerie had ordered the funeral director to bury the body as soon as it arrived. Harry's mother, his sisters Carolyn and Louise, his daughter Deborah and a score of close friends were baffled, hurt and ultimately outraged.

"Valerie didn't show up," Paul Winn said, still baffled years after the event. "She denied her mother, her sisters, her nieces an opportunity to say goodbye to Harry. When I asked her why, she said that she 'didn't want it to be a media circus.' But there were no media people there, just family and close friends. I made a list of the people who were there. I wrote down the time, and I made a note of the passages that the minister read over his grave and sent copies to everyone who had been there. I pressed a flower." To this day, Winn becomes visibly upset when he talks about the funeral.

Emery Barnes, a family friend, former Speaker of the British Columbia Legislature and member of the BC Lions Football team said, "It's the harshest thing I ever heard of."

Crest commemorating Harry Jerome's 1971 induction into Canada's Sports Hall of Fame

The event underlined and deepened a family rift that has left Valerie estranged from her mother and, in some measure, from others in her family.

Harry's gravestone, erected by Valerie at Mountainview Cemetery in North Vancouver, has an epitaph that reprises three lines (inexplicably in this context, as Paul Winn sees it) of the Robert Frost poem "Stopping by Woods on a Snowy Evening." Could it have been an echo of Prime Minister Pierre Trudeau's musings after he won his last election a couple of years earlier?

Winn still visits the grave on Harry's birthday. "I take a bottle of white wine with me. I don't know which end his head is at, so I pour a little wine on the ground at both ends. We have a drink together and remember the old days."

Of all members of his family, Harry was closest to Valerie. Early in 1980, they bought a house at 2552 Trinity Street in Vancouver. I found evidence of a will created at the beginning of February 1982, involving Harry and another woman, and filed, at the time, with the BC Division of Vital Statistics. A receipt from the British Columbia Division of Vital Statistics acknowledges receipt of a second Jerome will. Friends and family report that Valerie was named as the executor in the later will.

The tributes poured in:

> Harry's life was a sprint in duration and character. He crammed so very, very much into it. He was one of the most loving, giving, kindest human beings I've known.
> –Wilf Wedman, *Vancouver Sun*, December 13, 1982

> Harry Jerome represented the best qualities of citizenship. On behalf of all British Columbians, I want to express heartfelt sympathies to his family and many, many friends. His death was also a personal loss for me, as he had been a friend for many years.
> –Premier Bill Bennett, *Vancouver Sun*,
> December 8, 1982

The House of Commons voted unanimously to send its condolences to the families of Vancouver sprinter Harry Jerome and yachtsman Reginald Dixon.

–Moved by Joe Reid, PC, St. Catherines, Ontario

He was a beautiful runner to watch. He was so gifted, such a fine competitor, and he ran so smoothly. He was a delight to be with, always bubbling with ideas, always trying to improve things.

–Bruce Kidd, *Vancouver Sun*, December 8, 1982

He was like a son to me. It's hard to believe. I had just left him this afternoon. We were sitting around talking about all the problems involving Canadian athletics. Jerome grew from a boy with tunnel vision to a man who saw the whole community and all of its injustices.

–Dr. Auby (Al) Rader, *Vancouver Sun*, December 8, 1982

I join all the people who knew and admired him when I say it was not only a personal loss, but a great loss to sports.

–Bill Bowerman, *Vancouver Sun*, December 8, 1982

He was a Pied Piper with kids. They followed him, and they believed in him. He wanted so badly for the kids to have the things he had to fight for when he was a kid. The Premier's Sports Awards Program was his idea—and he's leaving a brilliant epitaph.

–Tom Walker, Executive Director, Sport BC, *Vancouver Sun*, December 8, 1982

It's a helluva loss. It's a loss for amateur sport in
this country because he understood it so well. People
misunderstood Harry—they thought he was bitter.
All he wanted to do was look for a better way if it
was there.
    –Brian Pound, *Vancouver Sun*, December 8, 1982

He legitimized track and field in Canada.
–Bill Crothers, *Vancouver Sun*, December 20, 1982

I should like to offer both my condolences and
those of the entire Olympic movement.
–Juan Antonio Samaranch, head of the International
        Olympic Committee (IOC) from 1980–2001

With his passing, we have lost this country's
greatest athletic achiever.
        –John Minichiello, *Vancouver Sun*,
                December 13, 1982

Harry Jerome's accomplishments have been well acknowledged
by his country. He was inducted into the BC Sports Hall of Fame in
1966. In 1971, he became a member of the Canadian Amateur Athletic
Hall of Fame. In the same year, he was named the British Columbia
Athlete of the Century and was made an Officer of the Order of Canada "in recognition of his achievements in track and field events in
Canada and abroad and for his services to fitness in Canada."

On May 28, 1988, a graceful, larger-than-life statue of Jerome
was unveiled at Brockton Point in Stanley Park. It has become a landmark, forever reminding the many thousands who pass by of Canada's
fastest man.

On June 1, 2001, his star was added to the Canadian Walk of Fame,
a stretch of sidewalk in the theatre district along Toronto's King Street
West. He joined such icons as Wayne Gretzky, Jean Belliveau and

A view of the larger-than-life statue of Harry Jerome in Vancouver's Stanley Park

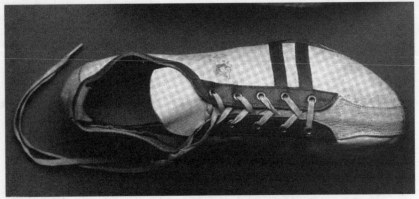

Pairs of Harry's track shoes are on display at the Bata Shoe Museum in Toronto.

Maurice Richard, Neil Young and Bryan Adams, Pierre Berton and Alexander Graham Bell. His shoes are in the Bata Shoe Museum in Toronto.

On July 15, 2002, Mayor Barbara Sharp of the City of North Vancouver, with Paul Winn as master of ceremonies and five-time Olympian Charmaine Crooks as a special guest, dedicated a large, well-equipped sports training centre as the Harry Jerome Recreation Complex. Brian Pound presented memorabilia that is displayed in the building. Sprawling over most of a city block, the centre contains training facilities for virtually every sport—hockey, swimming, track and field, wrestling—and is equipped with several state-of-the-art weight rooms.

There is also the Harry Jerome Sports Centre, a 53,000-square-foot velodrome and sports facility located in Burnaby, BC.

The weight room at the University of Oregon is named for him.

Prince Albert, Saskatchewan, Harry's birthplace, boasts the Harry Jerome Track Complex, built for the 1992 Saskatchewan Summer Games.

Since 1983, the Harry Jerome International Track Classic, the biggest and most prestigious domestic track and field event in Canada, has been staged in Vancouver. In 2005, Mayor Larry Campbell declared June 14 "Harry Jerome Day" in Vancouver.

Harry Jerome was a true romantic. But fate made it impossible for him to make his dreams of an everlasting love come true. His letters to Wendy when they were married, and later to other women with whom he had relationships, display a yearning for an idyllic, true love relationship. Towards the end of his life, promising her almost anything, he found himself in a sad relationship of unrequited love.

He was an idealist wrapped up in the body and spirit of a superb athlete with off-the-charts persistence and determination.

He was a loyal friend, a man and a hero.

Epilogue

*I learned to slip back and forth between my black
and white worlds, understanding that each possessed
its own language and customs and structures
of meaning, convinced that with a bit of translation
on my part, the two worlds would eventually cohere.*

—Barack Obama

Harry Winston Jerome, blessed with a perfect runner's body and driven by a compelling need to prove his worth, was born to be a winner. It's instructive to our understanding of him that, in runners' terms, his talent didn't blossom until relatively late in life. As he said, "As a juvenile, I couldn't beat anyone."

Harry came from a troubled minority family. But their trials and triumphs were not so different from those of thousands of other Canadian households. It wasn't until he was 17, in the fifth year of his teens, old as sprinters go, that he experienced the growth that transformed him from a gangly kid into a superbly smooth runner. By that time, the perplexing sense of being forever an outsider had surely rooted itself deep in his psyche. He was a Black kid stuck in a white world. His first, most devastating rejection came when he was still a vulnerable adolescent. But he was old enough to understand a situation from which his family could not possibly have sheltered him. Neighbours drove him and his family out of the neighbourhood. He had to be painfully aware, as he matured, that his father had spent his life working in a job that demeaned him, that his parents had wrenching disagreements about where and how to live and bring up their family, disagreements that led ultimately to family breakup. His self-defensive pride left him embarrassed when his only brother turned out to be marked by that terrible label, "retarded." His family was hardly a role model for marital success. His sister Carolyn left home at an early age. Louise spent part of her young life in foster homes. His only Black friend, Paul Winn, was so surprising self-assured that Harry felt diminished in comparison.

And then, figuratively, he woke up one day and had to begin the process of coming to terms with the fact that he was fast, really fast— so fast that the whole world would know his name. He must have been stunned by his God-given talent. He had already learned that acceptance was never a sure thing, that he would have to prove himself again and again. No one—not his family, not his friends, not his coaches and manager, and certainly not the sports establishment—could ever feel the pressure to excel or the pain of failure as keenly as he did. His whole sense of self-worth was wrapped up in the need to win.

All elite runners race against the obstacles in their lives. Harry hated to lose. His only option for success, in life and on the track, was to win, against all odds, and to win big. Everyone who knew him understood that losing at anything—chess, badminton, board games, cards—was an option he was incapable of contemplating. And while reality prevailed, allowing him to grudgingly concede when he had to at least pretend to accept defeat in ordinary games, his runner's body and his incredible need to validate himself gave him a hand equivalent to a royal flush whenever he stepped onto the track.

He learned to see his opponents as enemies. I don't think that Bill Bowerman, his Oregon coach, had to drill the idea of hating your competitors into his mind. Like his Olympic predecessor, Ray Lewis, who in every race ran against his bigoted high school principal and his coach, Harry was quite candid in declaring his "hate" for anyone he was running against. Losing only made him work harder, harder and harder, as hard as it took to prove to the world and, more importantly, to himself, that he really was a winner. There is no evidence that this "competitive hatred" went beyond the track. While, along with most of the people who lived in the high stratosphere of sports, he was not above doing things to "psyche out" his competitors, off the track, he liked and stood up for them. He was often a supporter and mentor of younger, emerging athletes. At the 1968 Olympics, Jerome was one of the athletes who protected swimmer Elaine Tanner,[28] another teenage phenomenon, when she was hounded by reporters after failing to win a gold medal. And Harry's friends stood up for him, coming fiercely to his defence when the press savaged him.

"Really good athletes are really quite self-centred," John Minichiello told me. "I don't mean self-centred in a negative way. He was good with his friends, but friendships wouldn't interfere with what he had

7

to do. The focus was running and doing well. He was self-centred a little like the way Ray Charles, in the movie *Ray*, is self-centred. Great athletes are the same way."

And it's no stretch to understand why Harry was, throughout his life, extraordinarily modest about his accomplishments. He was never a braggart. He understood that he could never let his guard down. He knew how quickly opinion could turn against him. The work and determination that took him to the heights he achieved were of his own making. But I'm sure he knew, deep in his heart, that his talent, the superbly tuned body that came as he entered manhood, was a gift, a blessing that changed his life.

How hard is it, in a highly tuned, well-developed athlete's body, to literally pull a muscle out of its mooring, especially a muscle as strong as one of the quadriceps? His own answer was simple: "I tried too hard."

It's true. The "big" races *were* hard; they did mean more. The real pressure was self-generated. Losing was not an option. In Rome and in Perth, notwithstanding the fact that there were extenuating circumstances—getting stuck in traffic and having to run to the stadium to get there in time to run his heat in Rome and going into the British Empire Games final in Australia probably running a fever, having forced himself to train with a mustard plaster on his chest—the self-generated pressure was crushing. Neither of his coaches, had they been there, would have let him run. But for Harry, losing was not an option. The censure he would have attracted had he taken himself out of the race weighed heavily on his mind. So he chose to run, knowing he was not at his best, but still believing that his will to win would overcome any deficiency. Better to give it his best than to save himself for another day.

Harry Jerome retired from competitive running at the age of 28, old for a sprinter, with an Olympic bronze medal and gold medals from both the Commonwealth and the Pan Am Games around his neck, and scores of prizes from track events around the world. He had been lauded for having made the greatest comeback in sports history. He mellowed and was beginning to teach his winning ways to a new generation of admiring youth. He had learned the stoicism that allowed him to deal with adversity by keeping his own counsel, by working twice as hard to succeed. And he always knew how to be a good friend, giving and attracting unalloyed loyalty. His solid core of long-time friends would go to the wall for him. Along the way, he developed small "p" political skills. He knew how to get the things he needed, how to garner support for his causes, for which he was becoming an increasingly articulate spokesman.

"Had he lived, he probably would have gone into politics," his friends told me. "And all of us would be there helping him."

A Loving Friend

Harry Jerome would have left an even greater legacy as an activist had he lived longer. As a young man, he went out of his way to avoid controversy, but in midlife, he knew how to pick his spots, how to use his fame to win his battles, to make things happen. He had already begun, at both the federal and provincial levels, to build a track record as a great motivator whose influence on kids could change their lives.

I've often wondered what kind of coverage the event might have had if he had lived to give the inaugural keynote address at the first Achievement Awards in March 1983, the Harry Jerome Awards.

He would, first of all, have been respectful. But by then Harry had lost a good deal of the reticence that had kept him from speaking his mind. He had a much clearer idea of what he wanted to do with the rest of his life. He would advocate on behalf of youth, particularly youth from ethnic minorities, and champion the need for inclusion, for facilities, for support for underprivileged kids in places such as Toronto. He would call on the sports establishment to be more balanced in their coverage and not build promising youngsters up, only to tear them down if they failed to meet expectations. He would have challenged the hockey establishment of the day to open the doors to Black athletes, challenging the myth that Blacks had skinny legs and did not have the ankle strength to be successful in hockey.

He would have expressed pride in the accomplishments of icons such as Lincoln Alexander and many others, but would have noted that they were still the exceptions that proved the rule. Above all, his humility and his realism about his place in the world would have won him a whole new group of fans in the Black community from which he had been more or less estranged for most of his life. And that might have added a whole new dimension to his life.

I wouldn't be surprised if he had been asked to join the board of directors of the Black Achievement Awards, perhaps under some other name. He, almost certainly, would have been a powerful force for equity in Canada.

I'm sorry I never met him.

Afterword by Dr. Brian Maraj[29]

When I was named as the head track and field coach at York University, I had no idea that 23 years later, different worlds would converge in Edmonton that would put a whole new light on my early coaching experience. That the Harry Jerome Awards came into being that year (1983) and that three members of my York University teams would win awards in the athletics category in 1983 and 1984 was a very special event at the time. However, with the writing of this book, this event of the past has taken on a totally different context that has a serendipitous quality. I first met Fil Fraser through a mutual friend in Edmonton (Gary McPherson) and things just went from there. We connected immediately during our first conversation at the Faculty Club at the University of Alberta with (film producer) John Verburgt. Fil told me about the book, and we discussed the idea of a "mythical miracle sprint" between runners from different eras. We had a long conversation that day, and many meetings followed.

Harry Jerome is an icon in Canadian track and field. Many Canadians will have heard of him either during his years of representing the country at international competitions or the younger generations, by seeing his statue in Stanley Park in Vancouver. Readers of this book will be exposed to the realities of sport and the life of the visible minority in this great country, as well as to the accomplishments, trials and tribulations of a man who tried very hard to be the best.

Track and field is the vehicle through which we make this journey and it has always been a world full of intrigue, glory and a certain amount of mystery. Most would agree that the 100 metres has always been a centrepiece in this sport. However, the central focus on the sprint has shown us the good, the bad and the ugly in this event over the last century, as the intense pressure of striving to be billed the "fastest person on the planet" can take a great toll.

Had Harry Jerome not won major medals on the world stage, he may have been known only as a flash in the pan, as someone who never really fulfilled his potential. But the remarkable resilience of this man to persevere in spite of his many detractors has provided the basis for a great and compelling story that needed to be told.

To compare Jerome's times with those of other runners, I created two set of factors, one that is additive (adds time to the runners' best time) and another that is subtractive (takes away time from their best time). The first two factors on the list are additive. For timing, 0.24 seconds is added to convert the hand times to electronic-timing equivalents, and the other factor is environment, which is added to Jim Hines' time, as he ran at altitude. Not all factors are applied to each runner. For the subtractive factors, I calculated a percentage contribution and used it to take time away from each runner's best (or baseline) time. One example of this is the time difference between 1964 and 1968, with the introduction of synthetic tracks as opposed to cinders. My calculation is based on the percent improvement seen by the change to the track, and the calculation is then applied to those runners who did not benefit from this type of surface. You will note that Powell and Bailey do not get very many (any) of the subtractive factors that are listed on the top row of the spreadsheet.

Once I did the run-through in applying the formula to all runners, Jerome and Hayes were tied for first place. I am impressed by the times of 9.75. The beauty is that their times are in keeping with the times of today (even bettering the world record). But I added one factor that broke the tie. I inserted a factor for serious injury, because I wanted to have all runners at their optimal level. I applied this to Jerome and to Crawford (he pulled up in the 1972 100-metre final). This factor represents only 0.001 as a proportion of the final time, but it was enough to have Jerome edge Hayes.

I thought that there were intangibles that we cannot account for as a function of time, so my idea was to subtract one one-thousandth of a second for every year from the present world record. Thus, one decade would equal one one-hundredth of a second. The advantage of this is that Williams and Owens would get more consideration for the era in which they ran. When the calculations were all said and done, all runners in the field ended up breaking 10 seconds.

Readers should be aware that my formulation is but one of many ways in which a comparison of runners from different eras can be made and is not meant to discredit the outstanding accomplishments of any individuals. Moreover, the calculations are by no means put forward as the unequivocal method for determining what could result from such a hypothetical race. I acknowledge in advance the possible challenges that there may be other factors that I have overlooked or the questioning of those that I have included as well as their relative contribution. However, my aim was to present what I considered to be the salient influences that would have an effect in creating equity across the decades for such a mythical sprint.

Appendices

I: Chart of Factors Used by Dr. Brian Maraj to Create a (Virtual) Level Playing Field

Name	Time	Final Time	F-Timing	F-Envt	F-Footwear	F-Surface
Asafa Powell (2006)	9.77	9.77	0	0	0	0
Donovan Bailey (1996)	9.84	9.84	0	0	0	0
Jim Hines (1968)	9.95	9.8913	0	0.13035	0.0199	0
Hazley Crawford (1976)	10.06	9.86	0	0	0.02016	0
Harry Jerome (1960)	10	9.73992	0.24	0	0.02	0.3
Bob Hayes (1964)	10	9.75	0.24	0	0.02	0.3
Jesse Owens (1936)	10.3	10.0147	0.24	0	0.0206	0.309
Percy Williams (1928–30)	10.3	10.0147	0.24	0	0.0206	0.309

Factored Times (rounded)

Name	Time*	Final Time
Harry Jerome (1960)	9.73992	9.74
Bob Hayes (1964)	9.75	9.75
Asafa Powell (2006)	9.77	9.77
Donovan Bailey (1996)	9.84	9.84
Hazley Crawford (1976)	9.86	9.88
Jim Hines (1968)	9.8913	9.89
Jesse Owens (1936)	10.0147	10.02
Percy Williams (1928–30)	10.0147	10.02
	*Minus 1/1000 sec for every year prior to 2006	

F-Coaching	F-Diet	F-Training	F-Physiology	F-Nutraceuticals	F-Injury/Fitness
0	0	0	0	0	0
0	0	0	0	0	0
0.04975	0	0.0995	0.00995	0.00995	0
0.0504	0	0.1008	0.01008	0.01008	0.01008
0.05	0	0.1	0.01	0.01	0.01008
0.05	0	0.1	0.01	0.01	0
0.0515	0.0206	0.103	0.0103	0.0103	0
0.0515	0.0206	0.103	0.0103	0.0103	0

Adjusted Final Times

Final Results	Time	Final Time
Harry Jerome (1960)	9.69	9.69
Bob Hayes (1964)	9.708	9.71
Asafa Powell (2006)	9.77	9.77
Donovan Bailey (1996)	9.83	9.83
Jim Hines (1968)	9.853	9.85
Hazley Crawford (1976)	9.848	9.85
Percy Williams (1928)	9.937	9.94
Jesse Owens (1936)	9.95	9.95

II: The Harry Jerome Awards

The Harry Jerome Awards have been important since their 1983 inception. Set in Canada's biggest city, where a couple of generations of immigration has attracted Canada's largest Black population, the awards were designed to provide encouragement and support to an ethnic group too often seen as occupying the bottom of the ethnic totem pole. Some 800 supporters turned up for the first presentation of the awards at a black tie celebration on March 5, 1983. Track star Bruce Kidd paid a personal tribute to his friend and running mate. "Harry was physically beautiful...he ran like the wind passing... a thrill to watch...a super friend, bubbling with humour and love," he said in an impassioned speech that brought tears to the eyes of many in the audience. He talked about how Harry used to go into Adidas, pick up a dozen pair of shoes and walk out again. Other athletes objected to this, until they discovered that he was handing out these shoes to Black kids who had no shoes to run in. Kidd told the crowd that Harry, after he retired, was so driven by the need to encourage kids to embrace a healthy lifestyle that he became a "fitness guerrilla." He would go into a school, give a demonstration and leave before officials discovered he wasn't supposed to be there.s

Dignitaries attending that first Harry Jerome Awards banquet included Governor General Edward Schreyer, Metro Chairman Paul Godfrey, Trudeau assistant Jim Coutts, Senator Ann Cools, future parliamentarian Howard McCurdy, himself a former track star, and future federal Deputy Prime Minister Jean Augustine, then a school principal. Also attending were future Ontario Lieutenant-Governor Lincoln Alexander, Toronto Mayor Phil Givens and Ontario Solicitor General Bob Kaplan.

Organizing committee member Hamlin Grange congratulated award winners, challenging them "to epitomize the determination and ambition that was at the core of Harry Jerome." Denham Jolly, who founded the event, pronounced it an overwhelming success.

But the event was ignored by the *Globe and Mail* and the *Toronto Sun*. The *Toronto Star* carried a picture with a caption.

But the evening was immensely satisfying to the 25 people who had attended that first meeting at the Underground Railroad restaurant on October 21, 1982. Bromley Armstrong, later an Ontario Human Rights Commissioner and Harry Jerome Award of Merit recipient, recalls being there. It was decided at that meeting to form an association and a steering committee that included Al Hamilton, publisher of *Contrast Newspaper*, Denham Jolly and himself. The name "Black Businessmen's Association" was suggested by Denham Jolly. However, at the urging of a number of women at the meeting, the name was changed to the "Black Business and Professional Association" (BPAA) as a statement of the organization's commitment to equity.

The first directors of the BBPA were Pamela Appelt, Bromley Armstrong, Jean Augustine, Jean Gammage (Kamala-Jean Gopie), Al Hamilton, Denham Jolly and Cynthia Reyes. Jolly, whose vision had given birth to the BBPA, was its first president.

Six Black Canadian athletes who had excelled at that year's Commonwealth Games—Angela Taylor-Issanjenko, Ben Johnson, Mark McKoy, Milt Ottey, Tony Sharpe and Desai Williams—were the first to be honoured at the awards.

In addition to the Harry Jerome Awards, the BBPA sponsors the Harry Jerome Scholarship Fund, providing financial support to African Canadian youth pursuing higher education. The idea for the Harry Jerome Scholarship Fund, spearheaded by Hamlin Grange, was realized through the efforts of Kamala-Jean Gopie, Pamela Appelt, Sheila Simpson and Beverly Mascoll. Under the leadership of Verlyn Francis, an endowment fund was established in 1996 and attracted corporate sponsorship. Today the fund awards some 30 scholarships each year.

Incorporated in July 1983, the Black Business and Professional Association is a non-profit charitable organization that addresses equity and opportunity for the Black community in business, employment, education and economic development. In addition to the Harry Jerome

Awards and the Harry Jerome Scholarship Fund, the BBPA provides networking opportunities for entrepreneurs and professionals.

The BBPA attained charitable organization status in 1984 and operates under registration number 108073503. Its website can be found at http://www.bbpa.org/.

III: The Records

March 13, 1959: North Vancouver High School, North Vancouver, BC
Jerome equals Percy Williams' Inter High School record for the 100-yard dash with a time of 10 seconds flat.

May 27, 1959: Empire Stadium, Vancouver, BC
Eighteen-year-old Jerome breaks Percy Williams' 31-year-old world record for the 200 metres, established at 22 seconds flat in the 1928 Olympics. He covers the distance in 21.9 seconds.

July 18, 1959: Winnipeg, Manitoba
Jerome wins the Canadian championship in the 100-metre race with a time of 10.4 seconds.

1959: Eugene, Oregon
John Minichiello takes Jerome to Eugene, Oregon, to compete in a meet against some of the better American sprinters. Jerome wins the 100-yard dash in 9.5 seconds, setting a new record.

July 16, 1960: Canadian Olympic Trials, Saskatoon, Saskatchewan
Jerome runs the 100 metres in 10 seconds flat, equalling the world record set by Armin Hary.

May 20, 1961: Bell Field, Corvallis, Oregon
Jerome runs the 100 yards in 9.3 seconds, equalling the world record set by Mel Patton in 1948. He became the first man to co-hold world records for both the 100-yard and 100-metre sprints.

June 15, 1962: Edmonton, Alberta
Jerome ties the U.S. National Collegiate Athletic Association record for 220 yards with a time of 20.7 seconds.

August 5, 1962: Toronto, Ontario
Jerome wins the 100-yard dash in 9.4 seconds.

August 25, 1962: Empire Stadium, Vancouver, BC
Jerome runs 100 yards in 9.2 seconds, equalling a new world record set by both Bob Hayes and Frank Budd earlier that year.

1962: University of Oregon, Eugene, Oregon
Jerome runs the anchor leg of the University of Oregon Ducks' 4x100 relay, setting a new world record of 38 seconds flat.

February 28, 1964: Portland, Oregon
At the NCAA trials, Jerome equals the world indoor record of 60 yards in 6.0 seconds.

August 8, 1964: St. Lambert, Québec
Jerome wins the Canadian Track and Field Championship in the 100 metres with a time of 10.6 seconds.

October 15, 1964: Olympic Games, Tokyo, Japan
Jerome wins the bronze medal in the 100-metre race with a time of 10.2 seconds. The feat is generally acknowledged as one of the greatest comebacks in track and field history. He runs fourth in the 200 metres, clocking 20.8 seconds, finishing just out of the medals.

July 15, 1966: Edmonton, Alberta
Jerome wins the Canadian Track and Field Championship in the 100-yard dash with a time of 9.1. The official timers huddled for 10 minutes before announcing the result as 9.1 seconds, matching the record set by his great rival, the American Bob Hayes. That record would stand until 1974, long after Jerome had retired from competition.

August 1966: British Empire and Commonwealth Games, Kingston, Jamaica
Harry Jerome wins the gold medal an injury had not allowed him to capture in the 1962 games. He matched his Canadian time, running the 100-yard dash in 9.1 seconds.

July 31, 1967: Pan American Games, Winnipeg, Manitoba
On a warm, drizzly day, Jerome wins the gold medal for the 100 metres with a time of 10.2 seconds.

August 11, 1968: Toronto, Ontario
Jerome wins the Canadian title for the 100 metres with a time of 10.5 seconds. Charlie Francis comes second with a time of 10.6 seconds.

August 31, 1969: Victoria, BC
Jerome repeats as Canadian 100-metre champion with a time of 10.5 seconds. Charlie Francis is again second. It was Harry's last official competition.

IV: Curriculum Vitae for Harry Jerome

Harry Jerome: Personal Information

Office:	Fitness and Amateur Sports Directorate
	Dept of National Health and Welfare, 365 Laurier
Home:	1081 Ambleside Drive, Apt 1306, Ottawa
Height:	5'11"
Weight:	190
	Single

Interests and Abilities

1. Understanding the forces that shape Canadian Society, especially with a view to utilizing the sports aspect of recreation as promotional, educational and informational means for encouraging greater involvement by all ages, particularly youth.
2. Conceptual analysis, demonstration and experimentation in communication techniques, especially regarding the adequacy and efficiency of traditional and innovative techniques for sports promotion.
3. Designing of and leadership in demonstration projects, educational activities on a national scale.
4. Public program design.
5. Promoting, lecturing and being a resource person.
6. Public speaking.

Employment History

Worked for Fitness and Amateur Sport, 1972, also sports researcher Nov 1968–July 1969

Phys Ed teacher, Vancouver School Board, Sept 1965–Nov 1968

Teacher, Richmond School Board, Nov 1964–June 1965. Taught math and science.

MSc Physical Education, July 1968, University of Oregon

BSc Physical Education, July 1964, University of Oregon

Teaching Certification, August 1968, University of British Columbia

V: Memorial Service Program

Memorial Service — Harry Winston Jerome — 1940-1982

**The Unitarian Church of Vancouver,
949 West 49th Avenue, Vancouver, B.C.
Saturday, December 11, 1982 - 2:30 p.m.**

1. Harold Brown - musical selections

2. Opening Prayer - Rev. A. Phillip Hewett

3. Readings

4. Leon Bibb

5. Friends of Harry Jerome

   Paul Winn

   John Minichiello

   Dr. Hector Gillespie

6. Leon Bibb

7. Friends of Harry Jerome

   Dr. Al Rader

   Wilf Wedmann

8. Piano solo - Stuart Parker - (Harry's nephew)

9. Concluding prayers - Rev. A. Phillip Hewett

10. Musical selections - Harold Brown

Ushers:

   Jack Brauckmann, Chuck Ennis,
   Sucha Gill, Keith MacDonald,
   Brian Pound, Gerry Strongman,
   Lou Mohan, Konrad Tittler

VI: Naming a Street for Harry Jerome

Minutes of the Regular Meeting of Council, held in the Council Chamber, City Hall, 141 West 14th Street, North Vancouver, BC, on Monday, July 23, 2001, at 6:00 PM

2. **Delegations (Continued)**
(b) Valerie Jerome, sister and Stuart Parker, nephew, and Paul A. Winn, friend of Harry Jerome
Re: Recognition of Harry Winston Jerome—File: 1085-03-S10
Ms. Valerie Jerome, sister of Harry Jerome, gave a brief history of the life of Harry Jerome. She also gave an update of the various dedications to Harry Jerome in other cities throughout Canada and the U.S.
She requested that the City of North Vancouver honour Harry Jerome in the community.
Mr. Paul Winn, friend of Harry Jerome, gave a brief history of the sports activities of Harry Jerome in North Vancouver.
Stuart Parker, nephew of Harry Jerome, requested that the City of North Vancouver honour one of its outstanding citizens, Harry Jerome.
Members of the delegation then responded to questions from members of Council.

5. Motions and Notices of Motion
(a) Recognition of Harry Winston Jerome, File: 1085-03-S10
Submitted by Councillor J.B. Braithwaite
Moved by Councillor Braithwaite, seconded by Councillor Perrault
WHEREAS Harry Winston Jerome moved with his family at the age of 12 to the City of North Vancouver in 1952;
AND WHEREAS Harry Jerome attended Sutherland Secondary School and North Vancouver High, graduating in 1959, and had residences in the City of North Vancouver for many years;

AND WHEREAS Harry Jerome is a household name in the City of North Vancouver as well as in the track and field community, not only locally but recognized regionally, nationally and internationally;

AND WHEREAS numerous cities and organizations have recognized Harry Jerome as a local as well as a national symbol of excellence in the sports scene and in the community;

AND WHEREAS Harry Jerome has been specifically recognized by a statue in Stanley Park, a sports facility in Burnaby, a fieldhouse and hill in Oregon, a national Harry Jerome award in Toronto, member of the Order of Canada, an inductee to the Walk of Fame in Toronto, member of the Canadian Sports Hall of Fame, founder of the Premier's Sports Award program and was the male athlete of the century for British Columbia in 1971;

AND WHEREAS Harry Jerome has brought great honour to his high schools and this community (City of North Vancouver);

THEREFORE BE IT RESOLVED THAT Council be urged to recognize this outstanding individual of this City;

AND THAT this motion be referred to staff and the Street Naming Committee for immediate action and recommendation to Council.

CARRIED UNANIMOUSLY

Endnotes

Foreword

1 Paul Winn is a Vancouver businessman and lawyer. He has served as chair of the board of directors of the Canadian Race Relations Foundation and as its Chief Operating Officer in 2005–06. His lifelong involvement in human rights issues, at both national and regional levels, includes membership on the British Columbia Human Rights Tribunal, management of the multicultural committee of the Law Society of British Columbia, senior policy analyst with the multiculturalism secretariat of the federal department of the Secretary of State and as director of the Office of Services for Visible Minority Groups at the Public Service Commission in Ottawa. Paul Winn is past president of the Black Historical and Cultural Society of British Columbia and a director of the Black Business and Professional Association of BC.

2 Brian Pound is a former athlete and journalist. He worked with the BC Sports Hall of Fame as communications director.

Introduction

3 Stepin Fetchit was a controversial actor who appeared in American movies during the 1930s. He portrayed a slow talking, slow-witted "coon," which offended Blacks, long before the birth of the civil rights movement. Stepin Fetchit was the stage name of Lincoln Theodore Munroe Andrew Perry. His portrayals made him a movie star who became a millionaire by creating demeaning stereotypes of Black Americans. Some, but not all, Americans regard him as the first Black superstar, who paved the way for others of his race.

4 The other man to hold both titles was American Bob Hayes, who equalled Jerome's 100-metre time of 10 seconds flat when

he won gold at the Tokyo Olympics. Hayes and Jerome shared the 100-yard world record of 9.1 seconds until 1974.

5   Many of them would have been surprised to know that a man many of their generation saw as a hero was the one to open the gates. John Diefenbaker, while prime minister, pushed the 1960 Canadian Bill of Rights through Parliament. One of its effects was to create a merit-based immigration policy that opened access to Canada from countries other than Europe and the old white Commonwealth.

6   The Citizens' Forum on Canada's Future, a Royal Commission chaired by Keith Spicer, was established by Prime Minister Brian Mulroney in 1990.

7   See "Black Like Me" in the January 1987, 100th Anniversary issue of *Saturday Night* magazine.

Chapter 1: Remembering Harry

8   It would have been a tough and frustrating choice. The first Black to play in the NHL, Willie O'Ree, described as the "Jackie Robinson of hockey," played for the Boston Bruins beginning in 1958. But it was 1974 before a second Black, Mike Marson, joined the league. In the 1980s, Grant Fuhr, the first Black to have his name on a Stanley Cup, joined the storied Edmonton Oilers.

Chapter 2: Roots

9   Newspaper reports of the era set his height at anything from 5'10½" to 6'. But Jerome's own CV put his height at 5'11".

10   *North of the Colour Line: Sleeping Car Porters and the Battle Against Jim Crow on Canadian Rails: 1880–1920,* by Sarah-Jane (Saje) Mathieu in the *History Cooperate.* http://www.history-cooperative.org.

Chapter 3: Not Wanted in the Neighbourhood

11   A certificate, dated July 1, 1956, reads: "This is to certify that Harry Jerome is eligible to compete for the *Vancouver Sun* Scholarship. The above-named person has served as a *Vancouver Sun* carrier-salesman for two full years and is, therefore, perpetually entitled, upon presentation of this certificate to the registrar of the University of British Columbia not later than September 10 of any year, to be considered an entrant, on the basis of matriculation marks, for the *Vancouver Sun* Scholarship. Selection of winners will be made by the university.

12   See *Some Black Men: Profiles of Over 100 Black Men in Canada*, by Rella Braithwaite and Eleanor Joseph. Scarborough, Ontario: The Marlon Press, 1999.

13   Sadie Hawkins Day, which occurred only on February 29, was a popular feature of the old *L'il Abner* comic strip. For teenagers in the 1950s and 1960s, it was a special day on which girls could take the initiative and invite guys out on dates.

14   Reported by Erin Ellis in the *Victoria Times Colonist*, May 5, 1989.

Chapter 4: How Fast is Fast?

15   "I didn't know anything about his sister," Minichiello told me, "but I would have taken anybody to hang on to Harry." It turned out that Valerie was also an excellent athlete.

16   Armin Hary, a self-coached, somewhat eccentric office worker from Frankfurt, ran the 100 metres in 10.0 seconds on June 21, 1960. He won the 1960 Olympics with a time of 10.2, a time that stood as the Olympic record until it was broken by Bob Hayes in the 1964 Tokyo Games. Hary's competitive career came to an end shortly afterwards, when he injured his knee in a car accident. He turned up in the news in 1981 when he was convicted of illegally routing Catholic Church funds to

a personal investment. See *The Complete Book of the Olympics*, by David Wallechinsky. Penguin Books, 1988.

Chapter 5: A Husband and a Father

17   The council approved two recommendations, which stated; "RECOMMEND that a grant of up to $500 be made in favour of Harry W. Jerome for the purpose of celebrating and honouring his outstanding achievements as a sprinter and that such grant be held in trust by the City Treasurer and used by him to pay medical, hospital and other proper expenses of Mr. Jerome in accordance with the regulations of the Amateur Athletic Association of Canada. AND RECOMMEND that Mayor W. Angus be appointed to represent this Council on a Committee which is being formed from Representatives of the District Council, Community Groups, the Amateur Athletic Association, the Vancouver Optimist Club, the Press Radio and TV Stations, etc., for the purpose of establishing an Athletic Scholarship Fund in the name of Harry W. Jerome, such fund to be used to award annually a student entering UBC that year who has displayed outstanding track ability and requires financial assistance to continue his or her education; AND FURTHER THAT the City Treasurer be authorized to receive public donations to the said Scholarship Fund and issue receipt for same, pending the establishment of a permanent Scholarship Committee.

Chapter 6: Mixed Media

18   For a good read, see *Neil and Me*, by Scott Young. Toronto: McLelland and Stewart, 1984.

19   Italics mine.

238 ～ Running Uphill

Chapter 7: "I Tried Too Hard"

20   Bruce Kidd did win one of Canada's four gold medals in the six-mile race. Others were Dick Pound (110-yard freestyle swimming), Mary Stewart (110-yard butterfly) and Harold Mann (light middleweight boxing).

21   We know that's not true. Elsie's father, Armie Howard, was a Black railroad porter.

22   American runner Ray Norton was one of the fastest sprinters in the world in 1959 and 1960. He held the world record for the 100-metre sprint at 10.1 seconds until Armin Hary and then Harry Jerome achieved a time of 10.0 seconds.

23   It should be noted here that Jerome had beaten Antao three times in races leading up to the British Empire Games.

24   Quoted by Hal Quinn in "Requiem for a Champion" in *Macleans*, December 20, 1982.

Chapter 8: "I'm No Quitter"

25   Bob Hayes of Florida A&M had just run the race in 5.9 seconds on February 13, but official recognition was still pending.

26   This is an obvious shot at Bill Bowerman.

Chapter 9: The Fastest Man in History?

27   Jamaican Asafa Powell is the new world's fastest man, breaking the 100-metre record on Tuesday, June 14, 2005. The sprinter ran the distance in a time of 9.77 seconds at a meet in Athens.

Epilogue

28   Tanner had longed to swim in the Olympics after watching the 1960 Rome Summer Games on television. Her dream came true eight years later, and she arrived at the 1968 Mexico City Olympics as a heavy medal favourite. She made it to the podium three times in Mexico City, winning two individual

silver medals and one relay bronze. But after being widely touted by the media as a favourite for gold, the results were disappointing for the 17-year-old, a disappointment that took her years to overcome. Tanner retired from competition following the 1968 Olympics at just 18 years of age. Her impressive career total included 17 national titles, seven Commonwealth Games medals, three Olympic medals and five Pan American Games medals.

Appendix

29   Dr. Maraj is the former Associate Dean, Research, in the Department of Physical Education and Recreation at the University of Alberta. He is consultant to, and will participate in, a television series on the impact of technology in sport, produced by John Verburgt. One program in the series will create a virtual field that will see Harry Jerome compete against the world's top sprinters.

Fil Fraser

Fil Fraser has enjoyed a long and illustrious career as a broadcaster, journalist, television host, program director and administrator, and radio, television and film producer. He is a member of the board of directors of Telefilm Canada and is chair of the Lieutenant-Governor of Alberta Arts Awards Foundation.

He is a Member of the Order of Canada.

Based in Edmonton, Fil is an adjunct professor of Communications Studies at Athabasca University. He is author of the best-selling memoir *Alberta's Camelot: Culture and Arts in the Lougheed Years* (2003).